# GERMAN RAIDERS

A history of auxiliary cruisers of
the German Navy 1895~1945

# GERMAN RAIDERS

## A history of auxiliary cruisers of the German Navy 1895~1945

## Paul Schmalenbach

 **PSL** **Patrick Stephens, Cambridge**

© 1977 Verlag Gerhard Stalling AG, Oldenburg und
Hamburg
Schutzumschlag: E. Beaufort
Gesamtherstellung: Gerhard Stalling AG, Oldenburg
English language translation © 1979 Patrick Stephens
Limited

**Frontispiece** *The auxiliary cruiser* Widder *passing through the Kiel Canal, followed by the* Atlantis.

First published in Germany by Verlag Gerhard Stalling
AG, Oldenburg and Hamburg, under the title *Die
deutschen Hilfskreuzer 1895-1945,* von Paul
Schmalenbach. This edition translated by Keith Lewis.

First published in Great Britain in 1979


**British Library Cataloguing in Publication Data**

Schmalenbach, Paul
   German raiders, 1895-1945.
   1. Armed merchant ships—History     2. Germany
Kriegsmarine—History
   I. Title
   359.3'2'530943       VM378

   ISBN 0 85059 351 4

Text photoset in 10 on 11 pt English Times by Manuset
Limited, Baldock, Herts. Printed in Great Britain on
100 gsm Pedigree coated cartridge and bound by The
Garden City Press, Letchworth, Herts, for the publishers,
Patrick Stephens Limited, Bar Hill, Cambridge,
CB3 8EL, England.

# Contents

# Preface

Innumerable books have been written about the German auxiliary cruisers, describing their voyages and successes in the two world wars. This poses the question of the necessity and justification for another book on the subject. I should like to answer this by saying that, after reading this one, the question is really why such a book has not been written before?

In text and illustration Paul Schmalenbach has filled in the gaps left by previous authors and given the first independent history of the German auxiliary cruisers from their initial advent to the end of their own war in 1943.

Herr Schmalenbach makes it clear in portraying the essential function of the 'auxiliary cruiser' weapon that success was possible only through the co-operation of everyone on board in a spirit of complete trust and discipline. More than in any other arm of the Services did the auxiliary cruiser operate alone, making her own decisions without direct contact with the homeland, often with little or no information, against a widely ranged opponent.

The German auxiliary cruiser, and this is conceded today by our opponents, waged a heroic and fair war at sea, such as has never been before and never will be again.

This book may serve as a memorial to all those men in the two world wars who did their duty on German auxiliary cruisers and performed their allotted tasks to the full.

BERNHARD ROGGE
Vizeadmiral (ret)
Commander, auxiliary cruiser *Atlantis*

*Model of the auxiliary cruiser* Wolf.

# Foreword

At the beginning of this book there appears an illustration of the auxiliary cruiser *Wolf*. This model, first exhibited in the City Hall of Hagen in Westphalia in 1918, deeply impressed me when I saw it at the age of nine. It was my first direct contact with a warship, albeit a model, and it strengthened my resolve to become a naval officer. I had many opportunities to reflect upon this model both as a cadet and later in the Indian and Pacific Oceans as watch-keeping officer aboard the *Emden,* then on the outbreak of war in the Atlantic as gunnery officer on the *Deutschland*. Here I learned about war against sea-borne commerce the hard way. Week in, week out, awaiting contact with the enemy, beset by political, strategical and tactical considerations and not least by the weather. As, during the course of the war, the names of the commanders of the auxiliary cruisers and their comrades in arms became known to me and I was numbering friends and colleagues among them, I began to think that the work of these ships should be collated to give a picture of their successes and failures. However, this should not be a comparison between the achievements of individual ships as no yardstick exists against which these can be measured.

When, therefore, in 1975 the publishing house of Gerhard Stalling asked me if I would be prepared to compile an illustrated book on the German auxiliary cruisers I was only too happy to consent. Accordingly I lay the result before the reader.

In doing so it has been my aim to give the little-known early history of the problems of auxiliary cruisers, taking account of their delicate position under international law, and to set down as clearly as possible the distinction between the respective usage of auxiliary cruisers by the British and German navies. Above all I have tried to differentiate between the ways in which they were used on the German side during each of the two world wars.

Life on board these ships revolved around the crucial role of the commander of each and the close co-operation existing between members of his crew, and I have tried to portray this with extracts from logs, photographs and sketch plans of encounters with the enemy.

In the choice of illustrations my preference has been for those which have not previously been published or which most clearly link with the purpose of the book.

I am grateful for the help of the following: Konteradmiral (ret) Kurt Weyher, commander of the *Orion*, for assistance with illustrations and notes; the Oberarchivräten directors, Dr Sandhofer at the Bundesarchiv in Freiburg and Dr Haupt at the Bundesarchiv in Coblenz, for the preparation of documents and selection of illustrations; Ernst Fröhling, Witten, for illustrations; Arnold Kludas for particulars of the *Normannia*; Hans H. Hildebrand, Hamburg-Bergedorf, for photographs of commanders and accompanying details; Korvettenkapitän (ret) Karl Schäfer, Altenholz, for information on torpedo technology and tactics; Franz Hahn, custodian of historical material at the Marineschule, Mürwik, for illustrations and documentary material; Peter Mickel, Hamburg, for the excellent and accurate sketches.

I have concluded the book with a look at the possibilities of a war in the space-age against sea-borne commerce with auxiliary cruisers using satellites and computers.

*PAUL SCHMALENBACH*

# Key to abbreviations

## 1  General

| | |
|---|---|
| det | Released or detached |
| K | Retained for cargo of coal and sunk after its transfer |
| P | Prize |
| + | Sunk (pages 18-20 = died) |
| (+) | Sunk by own crew |
| + × | Sunk in action |

## 2  Ranks

| | |
|---|---|
| dRes | From the Reserve of Officers |
| Adm | Admiral |
| FK | Fregattenkapitän |
| KA | Konteradmiral |
| KK | Korvettenkapitän |
| KL | Kapitänleutnant |
| KzS | Kapitän zur See |
| L | Leutnant |
| Res | Reserve |
| ret | Retired |
| VA | Vizeadmiral |

## 3  Shipowners

| | |
|---|---|
| ALL | Atlas-Levant Line, Bremen |
| A-S | Anglo-Saxon Petroleum Co, London |
| B & F | British & Foreign SS Co, Liverpool |
| Currie | Leith, Hull & Hamburg Steam Packet Co, Leith |
| DADG | German-Australian Line, Hamburg |
| DOAL | German-East Africa Line, Hamburg |
| GAL | Gdynia-America Line, Gdynia |
| Glen | Glen Line, Liverpool |
| Hansa | Hansa Line, Bremen |
| HAPAG | Hamburg-America Line |
| HSDG | Hamburg-South America Line |
| Laeisz | F. Laeisz, Hamburg |
| NDL | North German Lloyd Line, Bremen |
| OPDR | Oldenburg-Portuguese Line, Hamburg |
| RVF | Russian Volunteer Fleet |
| RM | R. MacKill & Co, Glasgow |
| Woerm | Woermann Line, Hamburg |

## 4  Shipyards

| | |
|---|---|
| B & V | Blohm & Voss, Hamburg |
| B & W | Burmeister & Wain, Copenhagen |
| Br Vulk | Bremer Vulkan |
| Desch | Deschimag, Bremen |
| Dobs | W. Dobson & Co, Newcastle |
| Duncan | R. Duncan & Co, Port Glasgow |
| DWH | Deutsche Werft, Hamburg |
| DW | Danziger Werft |
| FSG | Flensburger Schiffsbau-Gesellschaft |
| Germ | Friedrich Krupp Germania Werft, Kiel |
| GWT | Gouvernementswerft, Tsingtao |
| Ham | W. Hamilton & Co, Glasgow |
| How H | Howaldswerke AG, Hamburg |
| How K | Howaldswerke AG, Kiel |
| KWG | Kriegsmarinewerft, Gotenhafen (Gdynia) |
| KWK | Kaiserliche Werft, Kiel |
| KWW | Kaiserliche Werft, Wilhelmshaven |
| Neptun | Neptunwerft, Rostock |
| R & F | Ramage & Ferguson, Leith |
| SchiE | Schichauwerft, Elbing |
| Teckl | Joh C. Tecklenborg, Geestemünde |
| Vulc Hbg | Vulcan, Hamburg |
| Vulc St | Vulcan, Stettin |
| Weser | AG Weser, Bremen |
| Work | Workman, Clark & Co, Belfast |

## 5  Shipyards which worked together on converting vessels

| | |
|---|---|
| WB&V | Wilton-Fijenoord Schiedam with B & V |
| WOK | As above with Oderwerke Stettin with KWG |

## 6  Warship types

| | |
|---|---|
| ABV | Armed boarding vessel |
| AMC | Armed merchant cruiser |
| Bat | Battleship |
| L Cru | Light cruiser |

## 7  Merchant ship types

| | |
|---|---|
| F | Cargo vessel, cargo liner or tramp |
| Fi | Fishing craft, trawler, drifter |
| P | Passenger vessel |
| S | Sailing vessel |
| T | Tanker |

| | |
|---|---|
| WD | Whaling depot or 'mother' ship |
| WF | Whale catcher |
| WK | Whale factory ship |

**8  Hull & machinery**

| | |
|---|---|
| BHP | Brake horse power |
| DT | Displacement tonnage |
| GRT | Gross registered tonnage |
| IHP | Indicated horse power |
| kn | Knots |
| m | Metres |
| nm | Nautical miles |
| SHP | Shaft horse power |
| t | Tons |
| III Exp | Triple expansion |
| IV Exp | Quadruple expansion |
| Diesel/2 | |
| E-mot | Diesel electric |

**9  Nationalities**

| | |
|---|---|
| AE | Egyptian |
| B | Belgian |
| DK | Danish |
| F | French |
| GB | British Empire |
| GR | Greek |
| I | Italian |
| JA | Japanese |
| N | Norwegian |
| NL | Dutch |
| PA | Panamanian |
| PO | Portuguese |
| RU | Russian |
| S | Swedish |
| SF | Finnish |
| SP | Spanish |
| US | American |
| YU | Yugoslav |

# Picture credits

# The development of the auxiliary cruiser up to 1914

**1856** The declaration of Paris outlawed privateering, that is to say, the seizure of a belligerent country's merchant ships by private enterprise under the sanction of international law.

**1861/65** The American Civil War created a need for fast steamers either to impose or run blockades. This led to the speculative building in Europe of high-speed ships, which were purchased armed or unarmed. A merchant ship profile was retained as part of the deception.

A Russian naval mission which visited New York and San Francisco in 1863 took due note of these fast and armed yet inoffensive-looking craft.

**1870** The North German Confederation announced its intention of using merchant ships as a volunteer sea defence force which could be called upon to strengthen its very small navy, mainly in preventing reinforcements arriving from America for the French Army. There was bitter diplomatic protest from France, supported by Great Britain, and the Confederation abandoned its ideas for fear of impairing relations with the United States.

**1877** When war between Great Britain and Russia seemed imminent, the Russian Admiral Lissovsky recalled the vessels he had seen during his visit to America in 1863. He bought three 13-knot steamers on the stocks in the United States for use as auxiliary cruisers against British merchant shipping. Each was of 6,000 GRT, carried 15 cm (6-in) guns and had a cruising endurance of 20 days.

With the Congress of Berlin the threat of war receded. However, these three ships set the pattern for the state-owned 'Russian Volunteer Fleet' (RVF) which, in peacetime, was to link Black Sea ports with the Far East and, in wartime, reinforce the regular cruiser squadrons.

The Russian example was the spur for the first subsidy agreement between a government and a shipping company: the British Admiralty paid the White Star Line a considerable sum of money in return for which the company pledged itself to allow the Admiralty to become involved in the design of new ships, particularly with regard to the provision of gun mountings. All the German government did, however, was to make known to the two leading German shipping companies, North German Lloyd and Hamburg America, its wishes with regard to the design and fitting-out of their future express steamers. Both companies voluntarily agreed to accept any adaptations that were compatible with commercial considerations.

**1888/90** Four express steamers, the *Auguste Victoria, Columbia, Normannia* and *Fürst Bismarck,* were launched for the Hamburg America Line. Each was of approximately 8,000 GRT, 150 m in length and 17.5 m in breadth. They could achieve a speed of 18 to 20 knots and had accommodation for around 1,200 passengers. At certain points their decks were strengthened for the mounting of armament.

**1889** The first two British ships to be designed for a wartime role as armed merchant cruisers, the *Majestic* and *Teutonic*, were launched. They were very similar to the German ships. Subsidy agreements were concluded in France, the United States, Italy, Austria-Hungary and Japan.

**1892** The Russian government decided to build two types of ship for the RVF: a 19–20-knot passenger ship with a clipper bow and 15 cm (6-in) guns; and a 12–13-knot cargo vessel of 5,000/6,000 GRT, with extra large hatchways for the transportation of locomotives.

**1893** The first public reference to a German auxiliary cruiser was made: the mobilisation orders of the North Sea *Marinestation,* dated February 22, included instructions for the disposition of the *Normannia's* service and non-service personnel, which were to apply when she was taken over as 'supplementary despatch boat or auxiliary cruiser'.

**1894** The Naval High Command asked the officer commanding the Wilhelmshaven base how long it would take to have the four steamers launched in 1888/90 ready for service as auxiliary cruisers. The answer was five days. The work was to be done in the Brunshausen estuary by Blohm & Voss of Hamburg. The masts would have to be reduced in height so that the ships could pass under the bridges of the Kiel Canal.

**1895** The German Imperial Navy took over the *Normannia* at Kiel for an experimental 15 days'

service as an auxiliary cruiser. Her GRT was 8,716, she could achieve 19 knots and carried eight 15 cm, four 12.5 cm and two 9 cm guns; six 3.7 swivel guns and two 22-ton 'non-autonomous' torpedo boats each having a 45 cm torpedo tube.

**1898** During the Spanish-American War Great Britain raised no objection to the conversion of merchant ships into auxiliary cruisers.

The German government opened negotiations with shipping companies regarding subsidies in return for which ships would operate to an approved schedule. The first agreement required North German Lloyd, within reason, to make regular departures to the Far East and Australia. As part of the agreement, the government was to build harbour facilities, coal depots and, later, radio stations.

**1902** By this time the RVF owned six large and nine small ships built to standard designs.

**1904** On the outbreak of the Russo-Japanese War, two of the large RVF ships were moved from the Black Sea to the Red Sea where they mounted the guns they had brought with them and declared war on what they understood to be enemy commerce. The seizure of a British ship brought a sharp protest, causing Russia to release her and withdraw the two auxiliary cruisers. Great Britain consequently proposed that merchant ships should be allowed to be converted for use as auxiliary cruisers only in their own territorial waters. This met with opposition from all sides as various countries claimed the right to undertake such conversions anywhere on the high seas.

Russia deployed seven auxiliary cruisers in the war against Japan, to which their opponents replied

with 20 such vessels and 22 gunboats converted from smaller steamers. The Russians described their auxiliary cruisers as 'commerce destroyers' and the Japanese theirs as 'commerce protectors'. Russia also purchased the Hamburg America ships *Auguste Victoria, Columbia* and *Fürst Bismarck*, placing them in service respectively as the *Kuban, Terek* and *Don*. The *Don* operated in the North Atlantic but was sold in 1906 to the RVF and renamed *Moskva*. In 1909 she went to Austria-Hungary where, rechristened *Gäa*, she served as an accommodation ship for the German Mediterranean U-boat Flotilla.

**1907** The Second Hague Peace Conference issued 12 declarations, including one concerning the conversion of merchant ships to auxiliary cruisers: a converted ship was required to fly the appropriate naval ensign and her commander's pennant; she had to be subordinate to the belligerent power whose flag she flew; her commander had to be appointed by that power and his name had to appear in its appropriate service list; her crew had

to be under service discipline; she had to observe the laws and usages of war; and the ship's name had to be entered as a war vessel in the country's navy list.

No agreement was reached as to where conversions could take place, but all parties opposed neutral waters. Hamburg America and North German Lloyd committed themselves to signing on in the crews of their North Atlantic main line services a minimum number of personnel who had previously served in the German Navy.

**1909** The German government issued the 'Prize Ordinance' as an Imperial decree for the conduct of a war on commerce.

**1911** The Hamburg South America Line placed large express steamers on its River Plate route and likewise committed itself to the employment of a minimum number of former service personnel.

**1913** In accordance with the wishes of the German government the following conditions for new tonnage were agreed upon:

— Minimum speed of 18 knots;

— Fuel capacity to ensure a cruising range of 10,000

nautical miles at 10 knots, and space for all other stores to be provided accordingly;
— Twin screw propulsion;
— Improved sub-division, in particular a double skin along most of the ship's length;
— Adequate pumps and flood control;
— Two separate and independently operated sets of emergency steam steering machinery located below the waterline and protected by coal bunkers;
— Boilers, engines and high pressure pipes below the waterline and also protected by coal bunkers;
— Decks strengthened for the mounting of two 10.5 cm guns forward and aft and four 15 cm guns broadside;
— Increased number of coal-ports in the sides and decks to allow transport within the ship and to expedite transfer from vessels lying alongside;
— Stowage, pumping, flooding and cooling arrangements for ammunition;
— Preparation for the installation of searchlights and for the carriage of steam pinnaces, including provision for the necessary additional electric power;
— Taller masts for radio aerials and look-out positions;
— Radio installation designed for German frequencies.

As First Lord of the Admiralty, Winston Churchill decided to accelerate preparations for the conversion of British merchant ships to armed merchant cruisers. From 1914 onwards ships so designated were fitted with guns but were not, initially, supplied with ammunition. These

*The 'quartering ship' Gäa of the Austro-Hungarian Navy (ex-Moskva, ex-Don, ex-Hamburg America Line's express steamer Fürst Bismark) was from 1915 to 1918 an accommodation ship for the German Navy's Mediterranean U-boat flotilla. For most of this time she was stationed at Kotor.*

measures were undertaken during the period when the whole question of conversion at sea was being argued.

**1914** During the early part of this year 39 British cargo liners, mostly those carrying meat and grain from Australia and New Zealand, were fitted with a stern gun. The guns were there for all to see. By the end of the year, the number of armed ships had risen to 70.

German owners considered cancelling their 1898 agreement with the government for services to Australia and the Far East as these were really flourishing, but the matter never came up for discussion. On August 1 Germany declared war on Russia. The First World War had begun.

**Auxiliary cruisers in existence at the outbreak of the First World War**

| Country | No | 25 | 24 | 23 | 22 | 21 | 20 | 19 | 18 | 17 | 16 | 15 |
|---|---|---|---|---|---|---|---|---|---|---|---|---|
| Great Britain | 26 | 2 | | | | 5 | 7 | 2 | 10 | | | |
| France | 9 | | | 1 | 2 | 1 | | 1 | | 4 | | |
| Italy | 21 | | | 2 | | | | 2 | 1 | 16 | | |
| Japan | 4 | | | | 2 | 2 | | | | | | |
| Russia | 4 | | | | | | 1 | 3 | | | | |
| USA | 6 | | | | 2 | | 2 | | 2 | | | |
| Germany | 13 | | | 3 | 1 | | | 1 | 3 | 3 | | 2 |

# The role of the German auxiliary cruiser in the war at sea

The main German aim in any future war on enemy trade had been to paralyse it. Up to the turn of the century the enemies envisaged had been France and Russia. However, with relations between Germany and the British Empire deteriorating, the prospect of trying to cut imports into Great Britain began to be examined. It appeared possible that, in a global war, Germany might be able to force Great Britain to deploy her own regular and armed merchant cruisers to protect her trade routes. By this means the German High Seas Fleet's burden in the North Sea could be eased. This strategy was adopted in both world wars, but in different ways.

In the First World War four German auxiliary cruisers sailed at the outset for their respective areas of operations, whereas in the Second World War the initial wave was not despatched until six months after it had begun. When the *Kronprinz Wilhelm* made for Newport News in April 1915, the German war on enemy trade ceased until the following November when, after careful planning (which set a pattern for 1940) a second wave was sent out.

The experience gained by the unobtrusive auxiliary minelayer *Meteor* in enemy coastal waters led to her being fitted out as a commerce destroyer, in which role she achieved some success. This led in turn to a proposal that an ordinary cargo vessel should be equipped to serve as an auxiliary cruiser, and the fruitship *Möwe* was chosen. Such was the success of this pioneer that her name inevitably crops up whenever conversation turns to the subject of German raiders. In the guise of peaceable traders, ships of her type ranged the seas from the end of 1915, sinking enemy tonnage and ships known to be supplying him, creating confusion and delay. Also, many valuable prizes were brought home to supplement stocks of German raw materials. The same tactics were to be used again from the early months of 1940.

In 1914 German auxiliaries were able to rely on a well-prepared back-up organisation established in neutral countries, but from 1940 onwards they were supported by tankers and supply vessels sent out from Germany. In this context mention should be made of Soviet help and advice to the *Komet* during her arctic passage. Japan also lent assistance.

No matter how widely enemy cruisers and auxiliary cruisers were forced to deploy as a result of these activities, they found the German raiders hard to trace. The organisation behind their operations was difficult to break. Their overall effect might be difficult to judge but they certainly had a practical result as well as a popular and romantic one.

There were two basic differences between the German auxiliary cruisers and the Royal Navy's armed merchant cruisers. From the *Kaiser Wilhelm der Große* to the *Michel,* the crews of the German ships fought as destroyers of enemy commerce without thought of personal gain. The men of the Royal Navy's armed merchant cruisers, however, saw themselves as protectors of trade and shared in prize money awarded for their successes.

Secondly, the German raiders delayed and paralysed Allied shipping by their sinister presence as well as inflicting damage through their sinkings and captures. On the other hand, the task of the British armed merchant cruisers was to protect supply lines by intercepting the German ships before they reached operational waters or on their return. Their task was defensive.

The success or failure of any warship lies largely in the hands of her captain. The ship's morale depends upon his selection. Along with the co-operation of his crew, his character is critical. With his second-in-command he lays down the standard of training and his attitudes are passed on to the men by his officers and petty officers. Technical and material aspects are also vital and function efficiently only with a crew whose morale is high. In both world wars, the tasks to be done were faced with these qualities.

# Commanders and their crews

Only one auxiliary cruiser commander had been appointed to a converted express steamer in advance of the outbreak of war in 1914: Reymann of the *Kaiser Wilhelm der Große*. The others were called on in turn as required. Prior to the outbreak of war they had been serving on foreign stations and, because their small ships were unsuitable for a war on enemy commerce, they were then released to take command of the auxiliary cruisers as they were equipped and commissioned. One such man was Thierfelder, former navigating officer of the cruiser *Karlsruhe*, who took command of the *Kronprinz Wilhelm*. He was the youngest auxiliary cruiser commander of all and had under him a crew consisting of over 95 per cent reservists. The specially selected commanders of the cargo vessels which were fitted out later during the First World War to become raiders were very much more at home in their tasks.

## The Commanders

### Abbreviations

EL = Oak Leaves to Knights Cross
Plm = Order 'Pour le Mérit'
R = Knights Cross of the Iron Cross

+ U = Lost with his ship
+ ) = KA Kähler was awarded Oak Leaves for subsequent service

| Serial no | Name of auxiliary cruiser | Name of commander | Rank as commander | Date of birth | Birthplace | Entered navy | At age | Remarks |
|---|---|---|---|---|---|---|---|---|
| 1 | *K.W.D.G.* | Reymann, Max | FK | 8.3.72 | | | 42 | |
| 2 | *Cormoran* | Zuckschwerdt, Adalbert | KK | 1.1.74 | Worbis/Sa. | IV 93 | 40 | |
| 3 | *Pr.E.Fr.* | Thierichens, Max | KK | 11.3.74 | | IV 93 | 40 | |
| 4 | *Kr. Wilh.* | Thierfelder, Paul Wolfg. | KL | 23.2.83 | Rostock | IV 01 | 31 | |
| 5 | *Cap Traf.* | Wirth, Julius | KK | 23.6.75 | | | 39 | + 19.9.1914 U |
| 6 | *Berlin* | Pfundheller, Hans | KzS | 3.7.69 | Stettin | IV 88 | 45 | |
| 7 | *Meteor* | von Knorr, Wolfram | KK | 7.7.80 | | IV 97 | 34 | |
| 8 | *Möwe* | Burggr. u. Gr. zu Dohna-Schlodien, Nikolaus | KK | 5.4.79 | Mellmitz/Schl. | IV 96 | 37 | Plm 7.3.1916 |
| 9 | *Wolf (I)* | Hermann, Curth | KK | 11.7.81 | | IV 98 | 34 | |
| 10 | *Greif* | Tietze, Rudolf | FK | 13.9.74 | | IV 92 | 41 | + 29.2.1916 U |
| 11 | *Wolf (II)* | Nerger, Karl-August | KK | 25.2.75 | Rostock | IV 93 | 41 | Plm 24.2.1918 |
| 12 | *Seeadler* | Graf von Luckner, Felix | KL | 9.6.81 | Dresden | X 04 | 35 | |
| 13 | *Geier* | Wolf, Friedrich | KL | 6.6.80 | | IV 00 | | + 7.2.1920 Breslau |
| 14 | *Leopard* | von Laffert, Hans | KK | 25.5.79 | | IV 96 | | + 16.3.1917 U |
| 15 | *Iltis* | Brandes, Iwan | KL | 5.2.82 | | IV 01 | 35 | |
| 16 | *Orion* | Weyher, Kurt | KK/FK | 30.8.01 | Graudenz | IV 18 | 38 | RK 21.8.1941 |
| 17 | *Atlantis* | Rogge, Bernhard | KzS | 4.11.99 | Schleswig | VII 15 | 40 | RK 7.12.1940, EL 31.12.1941 |
| 18 | *Widder* | von Ruckteschell, Hellmuth also Michel, first cruise | KL/KK FK/KzS dRes | 23.3.90 | Hamburg | Res 09 | 50 | RK 31.10.1940, EL 23.12.1942 |
| 19 | *Thor (1)* | Kähler, Otto + ) | KzS | 3.3.94 | Hamburg | IV 14 | 46 | RK 21.12.1940 |
| 20 | *Thor (2)* | Gumprich, Günther also Michel, second cruise | KzS | 6.1.00 | Stuttgart | VII 16 | 40 | RK 31.12.1942, + 17.10.1943 U |

Kaiser Wilhelm der Große
*Max Reymann as Konteradmiral.*

Cormoran
*Adalbert Zuckschwerdt as Konteradmiral.*

Prinz Eitel Friedrich
*Max Thierichens.*

Kronprinz Wilhelm
*Paul Wolfgang Thierfelder.*

Berlin
*Hans Pfundheller.*

Meteor
*Wolfram von Knorr.*

Möwe
*Nikolaus Graf und Burggraf zu Dohna-Schlodien.*

Wolf (I)
*Curth Hermann.*

Greif
*Rudolf Tietze.*

| Serial no | Name of auxiliary cruiser | Name of commander | Rank as commander | Date of birth | Birthplace | Entered navy | At age | Remarks |
|---|---|---|---|---|---|---|---|---|
| 21 | *Pinguin* | Krüder, Ernst-Felix | FK/KzS | 6.12.97 | Hamburg | X 15 | 43 | RK 22.10.1940, + 8.5.1941 U,EL posthum 15.11.1941 |
| 22 | *Stier* | Gerlach, Horst | FK/KzS | 11.8.00 | Erfurt | IV 16 | 41 | |
| 23 | *Komet (1)* | Eyssen, Robert | KzS/KA | 2.4.92 | Frankf./M. | IV 11 | 48 | RK 29.11.1941 |
| 24 | *Komet (2)* | Brocksien, Ulrich | KzS | 6.6.98 | | VII 15 | 44 | + 14.10.1942 U |
| 25 | *Kormoran* | Detmers, Theodor | KK/FK | 22.8.02 | Witten/R. | 1921 | 38 | RK 4.12.1941 |
| 26 | *Michel (1)* | See 18 | | | | | | |
| 27 | *Michel (2)* | See 20 | | | | | | |
| 28 | *Coronel* | Thienemann, Ernst | FK/KzS | 7.11.98 | Gotha | I 17 | 45 | |

## Supplementary notes on commanders

(–) indicates the period of service aboard the respective auxiliary cruiser.

**1 Reymann** Section head in Reichsmarineamt (–) internee, prisoner of war, Reichsmarine: Chief of Staff Baltic Station, President Navy Peace Commission. Korvettenkapitän January 1 1921, Konteradmiral April 27 1923, retired list as Vizeadmiral, died July 10 1948.

**2 Zuckschwerdt** Commander gunboat *Cormoran* (–) internee, prisoner of war, retired list November 24 1919, 1940 recalled, 1942/44 Port Commander Languedoc, Admiral French South Coast, September 1 1942 special duties, May 31 1944 retired list, died July 1 1945.

**3 Thierichens** Commander gunboat *Luchs* (–) internee, prisoner of war, December 29 1919 retired list.

**4 Thierfelder** Navigating officer cruiser *Karlsruhe* (–) internee, prisoner of war, January 29 1920 retired list as Korvettenkapitän, Port Captain Stavanger, Haugesund, Staff Officer to Sea Area Commander Sandneshöven, died May 19 1941.

**5 Wirth** Commander gunboat *Eber* (–) September 14 1914 badly wounded and died in the water after the sinking of his ship.

**6 Pfundheller** Administrative head in Reichsmarineamt (–) internee, returned as administrative head in Reichsmarineamt, March 27 1919 retired list as Vizeadmiral, died December 25 1940.

**7 von Knorr** Naval Attaché Tokyo (–) seconded to Naval Attaché Washington, commander cruiser *Breslau*, Chief of Staff to commander of reconnaissance forces, October 2 1919 retired list as Fregattenkapitän.

**8 Burggraf und Graf zu Dohna-Schlodien** Navigating officer pre-'Dreadnought' battleship *Posen* (–) Aide de camp to Kaiser, retired list as Konteradmiral August 19 1939, died August 21 1956.

**9 Hermann** Senior gunnery officer pre-'Dreadnought' battleship *Oldenburg* (–) senior gunnery officer pre-'Dreadnought' battleship *Ostfriesland*, commander despatch boat *Blitz*, commander No 1 minesweeping flotilla, November 21 1919 retired list, died February 26 1927.

**10 Tietze** Officer on Admiralstab, Fifth Squadron, at the same time commander pre-'Dreadnought' battleship *Wörth* (–), died February 29 1916.

**11 Nerger** Commander cruiser *Stettin* (–) head of mining unit of High Seas Fleet, July 25 1919 retired list as Kapitän zur See, August 19 1939 retired list as Konteradmiral, died January 12 1947.

**12 Graf von Luckner** Watch-keeping officer pre-'Dreadnought' battleship *Kronprinz* (–) prisoner of war, Reichsmarine sail-training officer training ship *Niobe,* May 31 1922 retired list as Korvettenkapitän, died April 13 1966.

**13 Wolf** Chief officer *Möwe* (–) returned as chief officer *Möwe*, died February 7 1920.

**14 von Laffert** Chief officer pre-'Dreadnought' battleship *Westfalen,* administrative head in the operations section of the Admiralstab (–), died March 16 1917.

**15 Brandes** Chief officer *Wolf* (–) prisoner of war following sinking of his ship. Reichsmarine: *inter alia* commander of the naval arsenal Kiel, died March 1 1935.

**16 Weyher** Commander sail training ship *Horst Wessel* (–) Sea Area Commander East Frisia, January 1 1945 Konteradmiral, retired list 1947.

**17 Rogge** Commander sail training ship *Albert Leo Schlageter* (–) Chief of Staff, then Inspector of

Training Establishments Inspectorate, Commander of fleet training formations and the battle-group 'Rogge', March 1 1943 Konteradmiral, March 1 1945 Vizeadmiral. Federal Republic armed forces: as Konteradmiral Commander of First Defence Area, Kiel.

**18 and 26   von Ruckteschell** Commander minelayer *Cobra (-Widder, -Michel* first cruise) appointed to Naval Attaché Tokyo, died September 24 1948.

**19   Kähler** Commander sail training ship *Gorch Fock,* head of advance post units in the west (–) merchant shipping council, Commander of sea defences Brest, February 1 1943 Konteradmiral, died November 2 1967.

**20 and 27   Gumprich** Section head armed forces communications liaison with army High Command (– *Thor,* – *Michel* second cruise), died October 17 1943.

**21   Krüder** Adviser Navy High Command (–), Died May 8 1941.

**22   Gerlach** October 1 1933 rejoined Navy, 1939 commander experimental vessel *Uhlenhorst* (–) Sea Area Commander Peloponnesus, North Holland. April 1 1942 Kapitän zur See, died June 18 1970.

**23   Eyssen** Section head Navy High Command (–) head of Navy headquarters Oslo, Commander

**Above, left to right**
Wolf (II)
*Dr Karl-August Nerger.*
Seeadler
*Felix Graf von Luckner (Z.B.).*
Leopard
*Hans von Laffert.*

**Right**
Iltis
*Iwan Brandes as Kapitän zur See.*

Vienna 3 recruiting district command, April 1 1942
Konteradmiral, died March 31 1960.
**24  Brocksien** Chief of Staff commander North
Sea defences (–), died October 14 1942.
**25  Detmers** Commander destroyer *Hermann
Schoemann* (–) prisoner of war. April 1 1943
Kapitän zur See, died November 11 1976.
**26**  See 18.
**27**  See 20.
**28  Thienemann** Adviser Navy High Command (–)
section head Navy High Command, commander
pocket battleship *Admiral Scheer,* commander
maritime anti-aircraft regiment. Federal Republic
Navy: 1957/60 branch head Navy Command Staff,
October 17 1957 Flotillenadmiral, died June 27
1964.

All but one of the auxiliary cruiser commanders of
the Second World War were officers on the active
list. The exception was Hellmuth von Ruckteschell
who had been a U-boat commander during the First
World War. He carried out his duties so thoroughly
that the Allies brought him before a British military
court in 1947; he died in prison on September 24
1948. He served in the *Widder* and the *Michel*.

Three men, Kähler, Rogge and Weyher, had been
commanders of sail training vessels prior to the
outbreak of war. They had their operational areas
mapped out and took many of their former crews
with them to the auxiliary cruisers. The long-serving
commander of the survey ship *Meteor*, Eyssen,
took on one of the most difficult and challenging of
tasks, that of sailing the raider *Komet* to the Pacific
through Siberian waters. Six of the 26 auxiliary
cruiser commanders went down with their ships.

The commander received all reports from within
his own ship as well as orders from the *Seekriegsleitung,* radio messages and decoded enemy signals
traffic. His crew's reactions to discipline, monoton-
ous diet and boredom under tropical conditions
were also reported to him. He would certainly
discuss these matters with his 'Number One', his
administration, medical, navigating and communications officers, his head telegraphist and radar
operator and, last but not least, his engineer
officers. The prize officer would also be involved.
But for all this, decision making remained the
commander's responsibility and he had to have the
aptitude for running his ship and for coping with
the many human problems which could beset his
small world afloat, as well as technical, tactical and

strategical worries. No one could or would want to
take this responsibility from him. The enthusiastic
interest shown at postwar re-unions and the concern
for the welfare and problems of former crew-mem-
bers prove that the commanders carried out their
duties to the full. The courageous intervention of von
Ruckteschell's crew on his behalf when renewed
accusations were made against him (a belated and
unfounded act of spite) reinforces this statement.

Work began with the selection of a crew. Before
some of the ships were commissioned a substantial
number of men in each had to be replaced when it
became apparent that they did not have the special
qualities for the job. In the *Orion* the proportion
was more than two thirds. Irrespective of rank or
appointment, all on board were under the same
discipline and treated accordingly. A head store-
keeper, for instance, was reduced in rank for having
drunk one solitary bottle of beer from the stock
reserved for the men. Training and education
aboard an auxiliary cruiser were as fundamental to
the job as on a regular warship of equivalent crew
strength, such as a destroyer. The realisation that a
tour of duty lasting many months lay ahead, the
uncertainty of an eventual homecoming and the
breaking of links with family and friends, were
burdens which a commander shared with his crew.

To commission a ship which had been taken over
in a foreign port or at sea necessitated mustering a
crew from the personnel immediately obtainable.
At home, on the other hand, the crew could be
selected according to the ship's needs and available
accommodation. Unfortunately, complete details
of the crewing of auxiliary cruisers in the Second
World War have not so far been released. However,
many of the men were reservists, often from the
merchant service, while some came from the
original complements of the ships in their peacetime
trading days. Reliable figures are available for the
First World War: 104 Regular and 94 Reserve
officers, with 2,602 Regular petty officers and
ratings and 1,305 from among reservists. The table
on page 24 shows that only five per cent of the
*Kronprinz Wilhelm's* crew were regular Navy
personnel, an exceptionally low proportion.

Many types of technician or *Laufbahnen* (career
men) were to be found in a crew according to the
needs of a particular ship. A merchant ship in
peacetime did not need anything comparable to the
radio installation and staff which had to be carried
by a wartime auxiliary cruiser. Contact had to be

maintained with the home base and enemy radio traffic monitored, its type, frequencies and technical characteristics understood in order to discover his intentions as far as possible. This was the province of the so-called 'B' observation service *(Beobachtungsdienst)*. As well as intercepting enemy transmissions there was, of course, also one's own traffic to be coded and decoded.

Weapons are necessary for offensive action so the crew would be trained in gunnery and torpedo-firing. Many would have to be experts in the use of target and range-finding instruments and learn how to care for them, with the assistance of others already trained in their mechanisms. Minelaying called for its own brand of skill and those ships which carried aircraft would have to include a pilot, observer and mechanics in their complement, plus others skilled in the special requirements of any fast motor launch which might also be carried.

The crews always faced the prospect of casualties, either from direct contact with the enemy or through accidents. Nearly a sixth of the men who served in auxiliary cruisers in the two world wars failed to survive to return home. Taking the two separately, the proportions were a ninth for the First World War and a quarter for the Second.

**Above** *Officers of the auxiliary cruiser* Möwe *during her first cruise. From left to right, standing: Kapitänleutnant Wolf, First Officer (later to become commander of the* Geier*); Temporary Leutnant zur See Köhler, prize officer; Leutnant zur See Meisel, torpedo officer; Leutnant zur See Niedermaier, gunnery officer; Leutnant zur See (reserve) Wellensick, prize officer; Marinezahlmeister Schönwald, paymaster; and a former German colonial released from the captured* Appam *which had been taking him under escort to England. Seated: Marine-Assistanzarzt (reserve) Dr Pietsch, deputy medical officer; Korvettenkapitän Graf Dohna-Schlodien, commander; Oberleutnant zur See (reserve) Pohlmann, navigating and prize officer; Torpedo-Oberleutnant Kuhl, mining officer.*

**Right**
Orion
*Fregattenkapitän Weyher signs conferments of awards for war service.*

Atlantis
*Kapitän zur See Rogge bestows decorations on his men.*

Widder
*Korvettenkapitän (reserve) von Ruckteschell (left) during the distribution of Iron Crosses to his men by Kapitän zur See Bauer, Chief of Staff to the Naval Commander, Brittany.*

Komet
*Decoration of Konteradmiral Eyssen with the Knight's Grand Cross by General-admiral Carls, Supreme Commander of Navy Group North, Hamburg.*

**Top row, left to right**
Thor *(first cruise)*
*Otto Kähler.*
Thor *(second cruise) and* Michel
*(second cruise)*
*Günther Gumprich.*
Pinguin
*Ernst-Felix Krüder.*

**Above, left to right**
Stier
*Horst Gerlach.*
Komet *(second cruise)*
*Ulrich Brocksien.*
Kormoran
*Theodor Detmers.*

**Right** *Officers and men of the* Möwe
*at the termination of her first cruise.*

Wem Gott will rechte Gunst
:: Den schickt er in die weite

Die Besatzung der heimgekehrten „Möwe"

## The crew

| Serial No | Officers Active | Reserve | Petty Officers and men Regular | Reserve | Total | Died as result of enemy action Officers | POs and men | Total | Remarks |
|---|---|---|---|---|---|---|---|---|---|
| **First World War** | | | | | | | | | |
| 1   Kaiser Wilhelm der Große | 13 | 11 | 178 | 382 | 584 | – | – | – | I: 81 Spain, K: 503 Britain |
| 2   Cormoran | 13 + 5 | 4 + 1 | 325 | 5 | 347 + 6 | – | 7 | 7 | I/K: 346 |
| 3   Prinz Eitel Friedrich | 14 | 11 | 323 | 54 | 402 | – | – | – | I/K: 402 America |
| 4   Kronprinz Wilhelm | 1 | 19 | 39 | 408 + 36 | 467 + 36 | – | – | – | I/K: 503 America |
| 5   Cap Trafalgar | 8 | 8 | 118 | 185 | 319 | 4 | 12 | 16 | I: 303 Argentina |
| 6   Berlin | . | . | . | . | . | – | – | – | I: Whole crew in Norway |
| 7   Meteor | . | . | . | . | . | – | – | – | |
| 8   Möwe (1) | 6 | 6 | 223 | – | 235 | – | – | – | |
|      Möwe (2) | 5 | 6 | 223 | – | 234 | – | 2 | 2 | |
| 9   Wolf (I) | (16) | ? | (345) | ? | 361 | – | – | – | |
| 10 Greif | 7 | 3 | 130 | 167 | 307 | 5 | 92 | 97 | K: 210 Britain |
| 11 Wolf (II) | 9 | 7 | 247 | 84 | 347 | – | – | – | |
| 12 Seeadler | 1 | 6 | (57) | ? | 64 | – | – | – | |
| 13 Geier | 1 | 1 | (46) | ? | 48 | – | – | – | |
| 14 Leopard | 4 | 11 | 275 | 29 | 319 | 15 | 304 | 319 | |
| 15 Iltis | 1 | – | (73) | ? | 74 | – | – | – | K: 74 Britain |
| *Total First World War* | *104* | *94* | *2602* | *1350* | *4150* | *24* | *417* | *441 (minimum)* | |
| **Second World War** | | | | | | | | | |
| 16 Orion | 14 | 6 | 356 | | 376 | – | – | – | 1 accidentally killed |
| 17 Atlantis | 14 | 6 | 331 | | 351 | – | 12 | 12 | |
| 18 Widder | 10 | 8 | 346 | | 364 | – | – | – | 1 accidentally killed |
| 19 Thor (1) | 9 | 10 | 326 | | 345 | – | 3 | 3 | |
|      Thor (2) | 12 | 4 | 326 | | 342 | (12 killed in explosion in Yokohama) | | | |
| 20 Pinguin | 13 | 13 | 375 | | 401 | 18 | 323 | 341 | K: 60 Britain |
| 21 Stier | 8 | 6 | 310 | | 324 | 1 | 3 | 4 | |
| 22 Komet (1) | 12 | 8 | 250 | | 270 | – | – | – | |
|      Komet (2) | 14 | 4 | 233 | | 251 | 18 | 233 | 251 | |
| 23 Kormoran | 14 | 12 | 375 | | 401 | 2 | 78 | 80 | K: 295 Australia |
| 24 Michel (1) | 13 | 10 | 384 | | 407 | – | – | – | |
|      Michel (2) | 13 | 9 | 384 | | 406 | 16 | 274 | 290 | 116 in Japan |
| 25 Coronel | 16 | 3 | 331 | | 350 | – | 3 | 3 | |
| 26 Hansa | Did not actually enter service as auxiliary cruiser | | | | | | | | |
| *Total Second World War* | *162* | *99* | *4327* | *1350* | *4588* | *55* | *929* | *984* | |
| *Total both World Wars* | *266* | *193* | *6929* | *1350* | *8738* | *79* | *1346* | *1425* | |

## Notes
Numbers in the 'Active' and 'Regular' columns include an unknown strength of reservists.

Where no numbers are given under 'Died as result of enemy action', the crews returned eventually to German-occupied territory.

K   = taken prisoners of war.

I    = interned.

I/K = at first interned, then became prisoners upon American declaration of war.

+ before a number indicates that it is made up of personnel from German colonies and/or from other German merchant ships.

Coronel
*Ernst Thienemann.*

**Right** *One of the crew of the auxiliary cruiser* Atlantis *during the time she was disguised as the Soviet ship* Kim. *Each crew-member turned his cap-band back to front and added a red star above it.*

**Below** *Some of the crew of the auxiliary cruiser* Orion.

# The ships

**Above** *The North German Lloyd Line's express steamer* Kronprinzessin Cecilie *was designated as a stand-by auxiliary cruiser. She was homeward bound when general mobilisation was declared. She turned back for New York where she was interned.*

**Left** *The mail steamer (Reichspostdampfer)* Lützow *was likewise intended to act as an auxiliary cruiser but on the outbreak of war was detained in the Suez Canal.*

**Above** *The North German Lloyd Line's express steamer* Kaiser Wilhelm der Große *was the only one of the designated auxiliary cruisers actually to have been fitted out for the purpose in Germany according to plan. As a voracious coal-eater she had frequently to refuel at sea, the colliers tying up alongside her. On what turned out to be the last such occasion she was caught and fired on by a British cruiser, caught fire and had to be sunk by her own crew.*

**Right** *The express steamer* Cap Polonio *was fitted out as the auxiliary cruiser* Vineta *during the winter of 1914-15 and commissioned on February 8. However, on trials she was able to reach only 17 kts and for this reason was withdrawn from service.*

**Left** *On August 6 1914 the express steamer* Kronprinz Wilhelm *was met at sea by the light cruiser* Karlsruhe *which transferred to the liner two guns with their accessories and a small military support cadre. Within three hours the* Kronprinz Wilhelm *was ready for service as an auxiliary cruiser.*

**Right** *The North German Lloyd liner* Berlin *was normally employed on the run between Genoa and New York. The outbreak of war found her in home waters undergoing overhaul and she was thereupon sent to the naval dockyard at Wilhelmshaven to be fitted out as a minelayer. The photograph shows her in number 3 entrance lock, the wind forcing her against the side.*

**Below** *The auxiliary cruiser* Cormoran *interned in Guam. She was the former* Rjäsan *of the Russian Volunteer Fleet, captured by the famous* Emden *and fitted out at Tsingtao. Commander and crew of the ancient* Cormoran *named their little force after their inactive ship.*

**Above** *Trinidad Island (Brazil) in August 1914 and the gunboat* Eber *lies alongside the express steamer* Cap Trafalgar. *The* Eber's *guns and most of her crew were transferred to the liner, the* Eber *herself decommissioned and on September 4 interned in Bahia. The* Cap Trafalgar *was shortly afterwards sunk by the British armed merchant cruiser* Carmania.

**Above left** *The* Kaiser Wilhelm der Große *heels over. With a breadth of 20 m and in water 18 m deep at its shallowest part, her starboard side is still above the surface.*

**Left** *After a cruise crowned with success in the Pacific and South and Mid-Atlantic, the auxiliary cruiser* Prinz Eitel Friedrich *was forced to put in to Newport News, USA, through lack of supplies. She arrived on March 10 1915.*

**Above** *The auxiliary cruiser* Kronprinz Wilhelm, *the most successful among the express steamers, put into Newport News on April 11 1915, exactly a month after the arrival there of the* Prinz Eitel Friedrich. *She had in her bunkers 25 tons of coal, sufficient for two hours' steaming, and ten tons of water for 427 men, of whom 86 were down with scurvy.*

**Right** *October 23 1914 and the* Kronprinz Wilhelm *draws away from the North German Lloyd steamer* Sierra Cordoba *which had been coaling her. 700 tons were transferred, no small achievement between two ships rolling against each other in heavy swell. As well as 1,700 tons of coal, the Lloyd steamer had brought footwear, canvas overalls and messing utensils.*

**Left** *The auxiliary cruiser* Meteor *on her first cruise. The 15 cm stern gun is not yet mounted and her side alleyways are still open. This innocent-looking ship of typical British build aroused no suspicion and became the first cargo vessel to be converted to an auxiliary cruiser.*

**Below** *The auxiliary cruiser* Möwe *has just completed swinging her compasses and is about to pass through the Kiel Canal.*

**Right** *The auxiliary cruiser* Wolf *(II) in service. Having expertly laid 465 mines to destructive effect against enemy merchant shipping, she began her career as a true auxiliary cruiser.*

**Below** *The auxiliary cruiser* Wolf *(I) photographed from the pre-'Dreadnought' battleship* Ost-friesland. *On February 27 1916, on her way to rendezvous with the* Greif, *she stranded in the fairway off Neuwerk. She strained so badly that her engines could not be used and she had to be taken out of service.*

**Left** *The auxiliary cruiser* Geier *evolved from the* Möwe's *prize* Saint Theodore. *Captured on December 12 1916 with 7,360 tons of coal aboard, she was indeed a tasty morsel for her captor. On December 28 she was placed under the command of Temporary Leutnant zur See Köhler, retaining her merchant ship name and later became the auxiliary cruiser* Geier *under Kapitänleutnant Friedrich Wolf. On February 14 1917 she was sunk by her own crew who joined the* Möwe *for the trip home.*

**Below** *One of the only two photographs known to exist of the auxiliary cruiser* Greif. *As an additional disguise she was given a second funnel. She sailed from the Elbe on February 27 1916 having as escort a U-boat which turned back next day and was to have escorted similarly the* Wolf (I). *The impending departure of the two auxiliary cruisers had, however, become known to the British and lines of Royal Navy vessels were watching for them. The* Greif *broke through the southernmost line unobserved by the enemy but towards 0900 hours on February 29 they closed in on her. The* Greif *succeeded in sinking the armed merchant cruiser* Alcantara *but was herself sunk, blazing furiously amidships, by the combined fire of the armed merchant cruiser* Andes, *the light cruiser* Comus *and two destroyers. Her commander was the last to leave but was killed by shrapnel in the lifeboat carrying him.*

**Right** *The* Seeadler *set sail on December 21 1916. Strictly speaking she was not a sailing vessel in the understood sense of the word but a motorship, the sails being part of her disguise as well as extending her cruising range.*

**Right** *The* Leopard *was the first auxiliary cruiser to be lost with all hands. News of her sinking on March 16 1917 came initially from a message contained in a bottle which was picked up (and is now in the military archives in Freiburg) written by a group of her deck officers: '. . . in action with British cruiser. Fighting for the glory and honour of Germany. A last greeting to our relatives.' The time and place are given at the head of the scrap of paper and the addresses at the end. Not until after the war did it become known that* Leopard *had fallen victim to the cruiser HMS* Achilles *and the armed boarding vessel* Dundee.

**Above** *The Hamburg America Line cargo steamer* Kurmark, *later to become* Orion.

**Left** *The auxiliary cruiser* Iltis *is shown lying alongside the* Wolf (II), *to which she acted as a support ship. She was the former British* Turritella, *seized on the outbreak of war and renamed* Gutenfels. *She was to have laid mines in the Bab el Mandeb (entrance to the Red Sea) but it was decided to lay them off Aden instead. Here she was seen and pursued by the light cruiser HMS* Fox. *Action against the* Fox *with her superior armament could have had only one outcome for the former merchant ship and her commander's only alternative to a one-sided fight was to sink his own ship (March 5 1917).*

**Right** *The steamer* Santa Cruz *of the Oldenburg-Portuguese Steamship Co of Hamburg, lying alongside the quay at the port after which she was named, Santa Cruz de Teneriffe. Later she became the* Thor.

**Left** *The motorship* Kandelfels *of the Hansa Line of Bremen. She was to become the* Pinguin.

**Far right** *The Hamburg America Line turbine steamer* Neumark *which became the* Widder. *Of the German auxiliary cruisers which saw action during the Second World War, she was the only one to survive.*

**Below** *The motorship* Cairo *of the Atlas Levant Line of Bremen which became the auxiliary cruiser* Stier. *Although she sank her last victim she was herself so badly damaged in the engagement that she had to be abandoned and sunk.*

**Below** *The North German Lloyd Line motorship* Ems *of Bremen. She became* Komet, *the only German ship up to that time to have made the northern passage from the Barents to the Bering Sea. Departing from Bremen on August 19 1940, she was assisted by the Soviet icebreakers* Lenin *and* Stalin *into the Laptev Sea. Despite the ice she was then able, on the 28th, to transit the Sannilov Strait without the assistance of another icebreaker,* Malygin, *and the end of the month saw her off Bear Island in company with the* Lazar Kaganovich. *Reported enemy submarine activity caused the Soviet ship to turn back at the beginning of September but the* Komet *pressed on, passing through the Bering Strait on September 5.*

**Left** *The* Atlantis *in ice-bound Kiel harbour. The searchlights, light anti-aircraft armament and naval ensign indicate her military nature but not her exact purpose.*

**Below** *The* Orion *in home waters. She wore the dummy second funnel only when in the Baltic and North Sea. She is shown as* Blockade-breaker 36. *Her bow gun and the 20 mm anti-aircraft guns on the bridge are not concealed.*

**Right** *The* Thor, *in action on three occasions with British armed merchant cruisers.*

**Below** *The* Widder *off Bergen on May 8 1940. There is nothing about her to show what she really was.*

**Left** *The* Pinguin *in the Baltic in April 1940. She was engaged in training her crew in radar and torpedo work, and as a target-ship for other vessels whose crews were likewise being trained. The photograph was taken from the* Widder.

**Below** *The* Stier *as a 'peaceful merchantman'. What the British called 'degaussing' equipment is clearly visible. Fitted to many ships during the Second World War, it was a protection against magnetic mines and homing torpedoes. It consisted of an electrical system intended to neutralise a ship's magnetic field. A cable was contained in a covering of semi-circular cross-section which encircled the ship at the level of the uppermost continuous deck.*

**Right** *The motorship* Steiermark *being fitted out at the Friedrich Krupp Germania yard at Kiel.*

**Below** *The auxiliary cruiser* Komet *which made the most difficult voyage of all. Her commander had to sail through the Arctic braving not only the ice but Soviet suspicion of his innocent-looking ship.*

**Bottom** *In this photograph the auxiliary cruiser* Michel *presents, so to speak, her 'visiting card', a phrase originating in her commander's log. She does not appear in any way unusual, hundreds of auxiliary vessels carrying light anti-aircraft armament and extra deckhouses to accommodate their gun-crews.*

**Left** *The auxiliary cruiser* Kormoran *meets a U-boat at an Atlantic rendezvous.*

**Below** *The auxiliary cruiser* Coronel *in the Baltic at the end of her working-up period.*

**Bottom** HSK 5 (II) *was not used as an auxiliary cruiser but served as a training ship for a variety of purposes: officer reinforcements, and for* Ausbilddungsgruppe Front (AGruFront), *a training group for the U-boat offensive. On being handed over to the British (for whom she was being built in Denmark when seized by the German Navy) she was given back her originally intended name of* Glengarry.

# The planned auxiliary cruisers of 1914

By the time the First World War broke out, agreements had been concluded with the leading German shipping companies whereby 20 ships were to become auxiliary cruisers in wartime. Of these, five were to be 'first line' with their gun mountings already in position. Four were to be likewise prepared but held in reserve as 'second line' and another four, without the mountings, became 'third line'. The remaining seven, mail steamers (Reichspostdampfer) as opposed to the high-speed liners, were held available for employment as supply ships, despatch vessels, etc, rather than in an offensive role. Of the 13 ships which were to be used offensively, only six were available in home ports at the time of mobilisation, and two of these were handed back to their owners after a short period of service. Three ships were not commissioned at all, leaving only one, the Kaiser Wilhelm der Große, to be sent on her mission from Germany. Three avoided the clutches of the patrolling British cruisers by making for neutral ports: the Kronprinz Wilhelm (New York), the Cap Trafalgar (Buenos Aires) and the Prinz Eitel Friedrich (Shanghai). The latter was armed and crewed in Tsingtao from the gunboats Tiger and Luchs and then commissioned. Similarly, the Cap Trafalgar in the South Atlantic was equipped by the gunboat Eber. The Kronprinz Wilhelm met the cruiser Karlsruhe at a pre-arranged mid-Atlantic rendezvous. She had been sent out with armament and additional personnel to bring the Wilhelm's crew up to wartime strength.

By a stroke of luck the liner Berlin happened to be in Bremerhaven undergoing repairs at the outbreak of war. She was taken in hand by the naval dockyard at Wilhelmshaven and by the end of September had been converted into an auxiliary minelayer. She achieved the greatest success of any German minelayer when her mines sank the 20,000-ton British 'Dreadnought' battleship HMS Audacious. On the whole, however, her career as a commerce raider was disappointing. Not only was she beset by bad weather but an unfortunate circumstance brought her cruise to an abrupt end. Inexperienced interpretation of monitored enemy radio traffic led to her commander deciding, unnecessarily as it turned out, to make for a neutral port where she was duly interned.

The use of a high-speed steamer as an auxiliary cruiser meant heavy coal consumption, in the order of 240 tons a day. The availability of coal bunkers was dependent upon German supply lines, which in turn were reliant upon captured enemy colliers. This situation was thus a determining factor in a commander's course of action. After a few months the situation began to bite at the smaller auxiliaries as well. Not only did the liner Prinz Eitel Friedrich have to seek a fresh operational area but the even smaller Cormoran had to opt for internment. Faced with all these difficulties it is remarkable what the auxiliary cruisers of 1914 actually achieved.

## Ships which in 1914 had been designated for possible service as auxiliary cruisers

| Owner | Service | Name | GRT | Speed kn | Location on the outbreak of war and eventual employment |
|-------|---------|------|-----|----------|----------------------------------------------------------|
| *Ships in immediate readiness to serve as auxiliary cruisers—First Line* | | | | | |
| NDL | North Atlantic | Kaiser Wilhelm der Große | 14,349 | 22.5 | August 4 outward bound from Bremerhaven. |
| NDL | North Atlantic | Kaiser Wilhelm II | 19,361 | 23.5 | August 5 at New York. |
| NDL | North Atlantic | Kronprinz Wilhelm | 15,908 | 23 | At New York. Auxiliary cruiser equipment supplied by the Karlsruhe. |
| HSDG | South Atlantic | Cap Trafalgar | 18,710 | 18 | Sought refuge in Buenos Aires. Auxiliary cruiser equipment then supplied by the Eber. |
| HAPAG | Cruising | Victoria Luise | 16,703 | 18 | At Hamburg. Fitted out as auxiliary cruiser between August 4 and 6 but did not serve. |

## Ships which in 1914 had been designated for possible service as auxiliary cruisers—contd

| Owner | Service | Name | GRT | Speed kn | Location on the outbreak of war and eventual employment |
|---|---|---|---|---|---|
| *Ships ready to serve as stand-by auxiliary cruisers—Second Line* | | | | | |
| NDL | North Atlantic | *Kronprinzessin Cecilie* | 19,503 | 23.5 | Homeward bound but put back to Bar Harbor, Maine, USA. |
| NDL | Far East | *Prinz Ludwig* | 9,687 | 15.5 | Bremerhaven. |
| NDL | Far East | *Prinz Eitel Friedrich* | 8,797 | 15 | Shanghai. Left for Tsingtao to be fitted out as auxiliary cruiser. |
| HSDG | South Atlantic | *Cap Polonio* | 19,300 | 16 | Hamburg. Commissioned as auxiliary cruiser *Vineta* on February 8 1915 but served for only a few days. |
| *Stand-by auxiliary cruisers but not fitted-out as such—Third Line* | | | | | |
| NDL | North Atlantic | *George Washington* | 25,570 | 19 | Bound for New York. Remained there. |
| NDL | North Atlantic | *Prinz Friedrich Wilhelm* | 17,082 | 17.5 | On Spitzbergen cruise, sought refuge in Odde. |
| HAPAG | North Atlantic | *Kaiserin Auguste Victoria* | 24,581 | 17.5 | Hamburg. |
| HSDG | South Atlantic | *Cap Finisterre* | 14,503 | 17 | Hamburg. |
| *Mail steamers* (Reichspostdampfer) *in readiness—Fourth Line* | | | | | |
| NDL | Far East | *Bülow* | 8,965 | 14 | At Lisbon, outward bound. |
| NDL | Far East | *York* | 8,909 | 14 | Japan. Detailed on August 4 to be supply ship to cruiser squadron. |
| NDL | Far East | *Göben* | 8,800 | 14 | At Vigo, homeward bound. |
| NDL | Far East | *Kleist* | 8,959 | 14 | Padang, Sumatra. |
| NDL | Far East | *Lützow* | 8,826 | 14 | Detained in Suez Canal. |
| NDL | Far East | *Derfflinger* | 9,060 | 14 | Port Said. |
| DOAL | Africa | *Kigoma* | 8,156 | 14 | Outward bound, returned home round the north of Scotland. 1915 troop transport in Baltic. 1919 brought home the crews of the German warships sunk at Scapa Flow. |
| *Steamer not in line to serve as auxiliary cruiser* | | | | | |
| NDL | Genoa–New York | *Berlin* | 17,324 | 16.5 | By chance under repair in Bremerhaven. Minelayer and auxiliary cruiser. |

## Origins and builders

| No | Name | Ex-name | Owner | Builder | Date of build | Con-verted by | When converted | How acquired | Entered service |
|---|---|---|---|---|---|---|---|---|---|
| 1 | *Kaiser Wilhelm der Große* | | NDL | Vulc. St. | 1897 | NDL | 2–4.8.1914 | | 2.8.1914 |
| 2 | *Cormoran* | *Rjäsan* | RVF | Schi. E. | 1909 | GWT | 4–7.8.1914 | Prize *Emden* | 7.8.1914 |
| 3 | *Prinz Eitel Friedrich* | | NDL | Vulc. St. | 1904 | GWT | 2–5.8.1914 | | 5.8.1914 |
| 4 | *Kronprinz Wilhelm* | | NDL | Vulc. St. | 1901 | – | 6.8.1914 | | 6.8.1914 |
| 5 | *Cap Trafalgar* | | HSDG | Vulc. Hbg. | 1913 | – | 31.8.1914 | | 31.8.1914 |
| 6 | *Berlin* | | NDL | Weser | 1908 | KWW | 9.1914 | | 28.9.1914 |
| 7 | *Vineta* | *Cap Polonio* | HSDG | B & V | 1914 | B & V | 1914–2.1915 | | 8.2.1915 |
| 8 | *Meteor* | *Vienna/Brit.* | Currie | R & F | 1903 | KWW | 1915 | Detained at Hamburg | 6.5.1915 |
| 9 | *Möwe (formerly Vineta)** | *Pungo* | Laeisz | Teckl. | 1914 | KWW | 1915 | | 1.11.1915 |
| 10 | *Wolf (I)* | *Belgravia* | HAPAG | Work | 1906 | KWW | 1916 | | 14.1.1916 |
| 11 | *Greif* | *Guben* | DADG | Neptun | 1914 | KWK | 1915 | | 23.1.1916 |

| No | Name | Ex-name | Owner | Builder | Date of build | Con-verted by | When converted | How acquired | Entered service |
|----|------|---------|-------|---------|------|------|------|------|------|
| 12 | *Wolf (II)* | *Wachtfels* | Hansa | FSG | 1913 | KWW | 1916 | | 16.5.1916 |
| 13 | *Seeadler* | *Pass of Balmaha* | R. Plate | Duncan | 1878 | Teckl. | 1916 | Prize U 36 | 2.12.1916 |
| 14 | *Geier* | *Saint Theodore* | B & F | Ham | 1913 | – | 28.12.1916 | Prize *Möwe* | 28.12.1916 |
| 15 | *Leopard* | *Yarrowdale* | R.M. | Dobs | 1912 | KWK | 1916 | Prize *Möwe* | 9.1.1917 |
| 16 | *Iltis* | *Turritella* ex *Gutenfels* | A-S Hansa | FSG | 1905 | | 27.2.1917 | Prize *Wolf* | 27.2.1917 |
| 17 | *Orion* | *Kurmark* | HAPAG | B & V | 1930 | B & V | 1939/40 | | 9.12.1939 |
| 18 | *Atlantis* | *Goldenfels* | Hansa | Br. Vulk. | 1937 | Desch. | 1939/40 | | 30.11.1939 |
| 19 | *Widder* | *Neumark* | HAPAG | How. K. | 1930 | B & V | 1939/40 | | 9.12.1939 |
| 20 | *Thor* | *Santa Cruz* | OPDR | DWH | 1938 | DWH | 1939/40 | | 15.3.1940 |
| 21 | *Pinguin* | *Kandelfels* | Hansa | Weser | 1936 | Desch. | 1939/40 | | 6.2.1940 |
| 22 | *Stier* | *Cairo* | ALL | Germ. | 1936 | WOK | 1941/42 | | 10.5.1942 |
| 23 | *Komet* | *Ems* | NDL | DWH | 1937 | How. H. | 1939/40 | | 2.6.1940 |
| 24 | *Kormoran* | *Steiermark* | HAPAG | Germ. | 1938 | DWH | 1940 | | 9.10.1940 |
| 25 | *Michel* | *Bielsko-Bonn* | GAL | D.W. | 1939 | Dz. W. | 1940 | Seized at Danzig | 17.9.1942 |
| 26 | *Coronel* | *Togo* | Woerm. | Br. Vulk. | 1938 | WB & V | 1941 | | 12.1942 |
| 27 | *Hansa* | *Meersburg* ex *Glengarry* | HAPAG Glen | B & W | 1939 | WB & V | 1942/43 | Seized at Copenhagen | 1943 |

* Impressions of the service seal of the *Möwe* show that the name was spelled with a 'v', in contrast to later and present day references.

## Range and cruising endurance

| No | Name | Fuel (coal or oil) | Capacity tons | Speed kn | Range nm | Range at kn | Cruising endurance days |
|----|------|------|------|------|------|------|------|
| 1 | *Kaiser Wilhelm der Große* | C | 5,000 | 22 | 5,000 | 18 | 11 |
| | | | | | 17,000 | 12 | 11 |
| 2 | *Cormoran* | C | 2,500 | 15 | 13,500 | 14 | 40 |
| 3 | *Prinz Eitel Freidrich* | C | 10,000 | 15 | 10,000 | 14 | 30 |
| 4 | *Kronprinz Wilhelm* | C | 4,800 | 23 | 4,800 | 18 | 11 |
| | | | | | 17,500 | 12 | |
| 5 | *Cap Trafalgar* | C | 5,100 | 18 | 7,100 | 15 | 19 |
| 6 | *Berlin* | C | 4,000 | 16 | 4,000 | 10 | 16 |
| 7 | *Vineta* | C | 5,000 | 17 | 7,000 | 15 | 19 |
| 8 | *Meteor* | C | 4,000 | 14 | 9,000 | 9 | 41 |
| 9 | *Möwe (formerly Vineta)* | C | 3,441 | 13 | 8,700 | 12 | 23 |
| 10 | *Wolf (I)* | C | 5,900 | 13 | 30,000 | 10 | 125 |
| 11 | *Greif* | C | 6,000 | 13 | 35,000 | 10 | 145 |
| 12 | *Wolf (II)* | C | 6,300 | 10 | 42,000 | 9 | 194 |
| 13 | *Seeadler* | O | 2,100 + Sail | 9 | 4,000 + ? | 9 + ? | ?18 + ? |
| 14 | *Geier* | C | . | 12 | . | . | . |
| 15 | *Leopard* | C | 4,500 | 13 | 26,000 | 11 | 94 |
| 16 | *Iltis* | C | . | | . | . | . |
| 17 | *Orion* | O | 4,100 | 14 | 35,000 | 10 | 145 |
| 18 | *Atlantis* | O | 3,000 | 16 | 60,000 | 10 | 250 |
| 19 | *Widder* | O | 4,500 | 14 | 34,000 | 10 | 141 |
| 20 | *Thor* | O | 3,144 | 18 | 40,000 | 10 | 166 |

## Range and cruising endurance—continued

| No | Name | Fuel (coal or oil) | Capacity tons | Speed kn | Range sm | Range at kn | Cruising endurance days |
|----|------|------|------|------|------|------|------|
| 21 | *Pinguin* | O | 3,000 | 17 | 60,000 | 12 | 207 |
| 22 | *Stier* | O | 3,200 | 14 | 50,000 | 12 | 173 |
| 23 | *Komet* | O | 2,485 | 16 | 5,100 | 9 | 236 |
| 24 | *Kormoran* | O | 5,200 | 18 | 84,500 | 10 | 352 |
| | | | | | 74,000 | 13 | 237 |
| | | | | | 50,000 | 17 | 162 |
| 25 | *Michel* | O | 2,500 | 16 | 34,000 | 10 | 141 |
| 26 | *Coronel* | O | 2,600 | 17 | 36,000 | 10 | 150 |
| 27 | *Hansa* | O | 4,500 | 16 | 65,000 | 15 | 176 |

## Gross and displacement tonnage, dimensions and propulsion

| No | Name | GRT | Displacement | Length overall m | Breadth m | Drau |
|----|------|------|------|------|------|------|
| X | *Normannia* | 8,716 | 15,500 | 159.0 | 17.5 | |
| 1 | *Kaiser Wilhelm der Große* | 14,349 | 24,300 | 198.0 | 20.1 | |
| 2 | *Cormoran* | 3,433 | 7,250 | 104.0 | 13.7 | |
| 3 | *Prinz Eitel Friedrich* | 8,797 | 16,000 | 153.3 | 16.9 | |
| 4 | *Kronprinz Wilhelm* | 14,908 | 24,900 | 202.2 | 20.2 | |
| 5 | *Cap Trafalgar* | 18,710 | 23,640 | 186.0 | 21.9 | |
| 6 | *Berlin* | 17,324 | 23,700 | 186.0 | 21.3 | |
| 7 | *Vineta* | 20,576 | 24,500 | 201.8 | 22.1 | |
| 8 | *Meteor* | 1,912 | 3,640 | 89.1 | 11.3 | |
| 9 | *Möwe* | 4,788 | 9,800 | 123.7 | 14.4 | |
| 10 | *Wolf (I)* | 6,648 | 12,900 | 141.1 | 16.2 | |
| 11 | *Greif* | 4,962 | 9,900 | 131.7 | 16.4 | |
| 12 | *Wolf (II)* | 5,809 | 14,200 | 135.0 | 17.1 | |
| 13 | *Seeadler* | 1,571 | 4,500 | 83.5 | 11.8 | |
| 14 | *Geier* | 4,992 | 9,700 | 127.2 | 15.8 | |
| 15 | *Leopard* | 4,652 | 9,800 | 124.7 | 15.8 | |
| 16 | *Iltis* | 5,528 | 1,070 | 135.2 | 16.9 | |
| 17 | *Orion* | 7,021 | 15,700 | 148 | 18.6 | |
| 18 | *Atlantis* | 7,862 | 17,600 | 155 | 18.7 | |
| 19 | *Widder* | 7,851 | 16,800 | 152 | 18.2 | |
| 20 | *Thor* | 3,862 | 9,200 | 122 | 16.7 | |
| 21 | *Pinguin* | 7,766 | 17,600 | 155 | 18.7 | |
| 22 | *Stier* | 4,778 | 11,000 | 134 | 17.3 | |
| 23 | *Komet* | 3,287 | 7,500 | 115 | 15.3 | |
| 24 | *Kormoran* | 8,736 | 19,900 | 164 | 20.2 | |
| 25 | *Michel* | 4,740 | 10,900 | 132 | 16.8 | |
| 26 | *Coronel* | 5,042 | 12,700 | 134 | 17.9 | |
| 27 | *Hansa* | 9,138 | 19,200 | 153 | 20.1 | |

## References to and names of the German auxiliary cruisers of the Second World War

| Heavy or light | Aux cruiser no | Ship no | Name | Reference in British intelligence reports | Successive commanders |
|---|---|---|---|---|---|
| H | 1 | 36 | *Orion* | Raider A | Weyher |
| H | 2 | 16 | *Atlantis* | Raider C | Rogge |
| H | 3 | 21 | *Widder* | Raider D | v.Ruckteschell |
| L | 4 | 10 | *Thor* | Raider E | Kähler, Gumprich |
| H | 5 | 33 | *Pinguin* | Raider F | Krüder |
| L | 6 | 23 | *Stier* | Raider J | Gerlach |
| L | 7 | 45 | *Komet* | Raider B | Eyssen, Brocksien |
| H | 8 | 41 | *Kormoran* | Raider G | Detmers |
| H | 9 | 28 | *Michel* | Raider H | v.Ruckteschell, Gumprich |
| H | 10 | 14 | *Coronel* | | Thienemann |
| H | 5 | | | | Henigst |

| board m | HP* | Speed kn | Type | No of decks | No of holds | Sub-division (Compartments) | Propulsion (B = boilers) | Propellers |
|---|---|---|---|---|---|---|---|---|
| 10.5 | 14,000 | 20 | P | 4 | | 11 | 2 3-cyl-III Exp B: 6 | 2 |
| 11.9 | 28,000 | 22.5 | P | 4 | | 16 | 2 3-cyl-III Exp B:14 | 2 |
| 9.2 | 4,750 | 13 | F | 3 | 4 | 8 | 1 3-cyl-III Exp B: 4 | 1 |
| 9.8 | 7,000 | 15 | P | 3 | | 9 | 2 4-cyl-IV Exp B: 4 | 2 |
| 11.9 | 36,000 | 23 | P | 4 | | 17 | 2 6-cyl-IV Exp B:16 | 2 |
| 13.4 | | 18 | P | 4 | | 12 | 2 4-cyl-III Exp T** B: 14 | 2 |
| 11.8 | 14,000 | 16.5 | P | 4 | | 11 | 2 4-cyl-IV Exp B: 7 | 2 |
| 13.3 | 16,000 | 16.9 | P | 4 | | 12 | 2 3-cyl-III Exp T** B: 14 | 2 |
| 5.4 | 2,400 | 14 | F | 2 | 2 | 7 | 1 3-cyl-III Exp B: 2 | 1 |
| 9.9 | 3,200 | 13.3 | F | 4 | 4 | 4 | 1 3-cyl-III Exp B: 5 | 1 |
| 9.7 | 3,300 | 13 | F | 4 | 3 | 9 | 1 4-cyl-IV Exp B: 4 | 1 |
| 8.1 | 3,000 | 13 | F | 5 | 2 | 7 | 1 3-cyl-III Exp B: 2 | 1 |
| 9.0 | 2,800 | 10.5 | F | 5 | 2 | 7 | 1 3-cyl-III Exp B: 3 | 1 |
| 8.2 | 900 | 9 | F | 4 | 2 | 5 | 1 4-cyl-Diesel | 1 |
| 8.3 | 1,800 | 12.6 | F | 4 | 2 | 7 | 1 3-cyl-III Exp B: 2 | 1 |
| 8.1 | 2,400 | 13 | F | 5 | 2 | 7 | 1 3-cyl-III Exp B: 2 | 1 |
| | 2,600 | 11 | F | 5 | 2 | 7 | 1 4-cyl-IV Exp B: 3 | 1 |
| 12.1 | 6,200 | 14 | F | 2 | 6 | 9 | 1 geared turbine B: 4 | 1 |
| 10.2 | 7,600 | 16 | F | 2 | 6 | 8 | 2 6-cyl-Diesel | 1 |
| 12.2 | 6,200 | 14 | F | 2 | 6 | 9 | 1 geared turbine B: 4 | 1 |
| 10.5 | 6,500 | 18 | F | 3 | 4 | 7 | 1 geared turbine B: 4 | 1 |
| 10.2 | 7,600 | 17 | F | 2 | 6 | 7 | 2 6-cyl-Diesel | 1 |
| 10.3 | 3,750 | 14 | F | 2 | 5 | 7 | 1 7-cyl-Diesel | 1 |
| 6.8 | 3,900 | 16 | F | 1 | 4 | 7 | 2 6-cyl-Diesel | 1 |
| 12.9 | 16,000 | 18 | F | 3 | 6 | 6 | 4 9-cyl-Diesel/2 E-Mot. | 1 |
| | 6,650 | 16 | F | 2 | 5 | 8 | 2 8-cyl-Diesel | 1 |
| 12.9 | 5,100 | 16 | F | 3 | 6 | 6 | 4 9-cyl-Diesel | 1 |
| | 9,000 | 17 | F | 3 | 6 | . | 2 6-cyl-Diesel | 1 |

* Reciprocating engines = IHP; Turbines = SHP; Diesels = BHP.
** III exp T = triple expansion machinery with low pressure turbine.

# Equipment for war

## Disguise and deception

An auxiliary cruiser fulfilled her role if she succeeded in a) maintaining her deceptively peaceful character until the last moment, and b) gained a position to enforce her will, with due regard to the laws and usages of war. It was all the better if she was disguised to resemble a particular vessel customarily seen in a particular area. In other words, if an interception was to be successful, weapons necessary to the fulfilment of the second part of her role had to be concealed through fulfilment of the first.

Everything possible had to be done to conceal the auxiliary cruiser's hostile intent. To the observer she had to appear a merchant vessel, the warship trappings hidden.

If the commander of an auxiliary cruiser was going to deceive the masters of other ships, he had to give the matter a great deal of thought and ensure adequate preparations, including crew drill. His course, for one thing, had to be acceptable and usual for the appropriate part of the world. The standard of cleanliness could identify some companies' ships. Others favoured a particular builder whose characteristics remained long after a ship had changed hands. The *Pinguin* met her end because the pilot of the British cruiser *Cornwall*'s scout plane reported that he could not see any coloured men about her decks; this would have been the case with a genuine British cargo vessel, which the *Pinguin* was trying to pass herself off as. Deception was not just a matter of external appearance. Slowness in answering a hail, a certain air of indifference and sometimes a degree of slovenliness, all helped to deceive even the most observant shipmaster.

Above all, the ship's military fittings had to be so disguised that they could not be detected until they were revealed at the decisive moment. Accordingly, guns, torpedo tubes and light armament were either camouflaged thoroughly or their outlines built over. Pictures show how this was done: dummy bulkheads, hinged plating to fall away to give a clear arc of fire, using either springs or counterweights, guns covered with cabledrums or locomotive fireboxes, and so on. There was no limit to inventiveness but it all had to disappear with lightning speed when the ship went into action.

When simulating a ship belonging to a particular company, all that company's characteristics had to be perfected, and the many former merchant service officers aboard the auxiliary cruisers were able to help in this. The positions of masts, derrick posts and boats might have to be altered and bulwarks raised to give the impression of a continuous deck instead of wells. Funnel markings would have to be altered and topmasts raised or lowered. Hull and superstructure would probably have to be repainted, and many other factors taken into account if successful camouflage was to be achieved. The enemy expected neutral ships to have their names, ports of registry and national flags painted on their sides and this had to be remembered. All in all, a substantial part of the auxiliary cruiser's war was waged with welding torch, saw and paintbrush. At night, when the danger in making these conversions was minimised, a ship could appear half Ben Line, half Bank Line. If the recognition features of one company were to be seen with those of another on the same vessel, the average merchant ship captain would probably have radioed a report on what he considered to be a rather peculiar craft. Whereupon, if an expression from the hunting field may be permitted, the quarry would have to 'go to earth'.

**Above** *The* Orion *disguised as the Dutch* Beemsterdijk.

**Right** *The* Orion *increased her freeboard using sheet metal added forward of the bridge structure.*

**Above** *The* Orion *disguised to represent a Brazilian ship, the* Mandu.

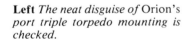

**Left** *The neat disguise of* Orion's *port triple torpedo mounting is checked.*

**Left** *The* Orion's *forward derrick posts are shortened to give her an altered profile and thus out-date any description of her which the enemy may have circulated for recognition purposes.*

**Above** *The* Orion *with only one short instead of two tall derrick posts.*

**Right** *The* Orion *as a Swede, with freeboard altered to make her almost a flush-decker. Metal triangles against the vertical funnel give the impression of rake from a distance. The Swedish flag, the word* SVERIGE *(Swedish) on the hull and the peacetime painting of it and of the superstructure and funnel all help to disguise the* Orion's *real purpose.*

## Armament

Guns were the only weapons on board those auxiliary cruisers commissioned under the mobilisation of 1914, although in September of that year the *Berlin* was equipped for minelaying, as was the *Meteor* in 1915. Each had two torpedo tubes for close-range action, and the *Meteor* used hers to good effect against the British armed boarding vessel *The Ramsey*. Minelaying played an important part from the commencement of the *Möwe*'s and *Wolf*'s operations.

## Gunnery

Considering the second-class material which had been put aside for their use on mobilisation, it is hardly surprising that the auxiliary cruisers of 1914 achieved only limited success. In fact, ammunition shortage reduced the *Kronprinz Wilhelm* to having to ram her victims in order to sink them! During both world wars the auxiliary cruiser was regarded as a second best compared with the regular cruiser. Fire control arrangements were primitive, but simple and robust, and relied for the most part on telephone contact between the gunnery officer and the guns. Some distance and deflection measuring instruments were provided but, up to the commissioning of the *Wolf*, the auxiliary cruiser's

main technical aids were a stereoscopic rangefinder and electric target-setting. During the Second World War matters improved with electrical expertise and modern apparatus. Up to the Second World War, however, gunnery material remained 'second choice', although modern medium and light anti-aircraft guns were supplied to the ships in accordance with the demands of the time. The 3- and 6-cm anti-tank guns selected as support weapons were a decided blunder, although the result of the best of intentions. The main weight of 15-cm armament during the Second World War came from one or other of the pre-'Dreadnought' battleships *Schlesien* or *Schleswig-Holstein*, after they had been given a good overhaul. How these out-dated weapons matched up to what was hoped for from them, or what their effect was on the relatively soft hulls upon which they were mounted, we shall never know.

Types and quantities of ammunition would seem to have been suited to needs. The necessity for ammunition storage at an even temperature and below the waterline to minimise the danger of fire had been realised by 1939 and means of accelerating its transport from magazine to firing positions were being continually improved.

Boarding parties and prize crews were provided from the beginning with personal protection (rifles, pistols and, as available, automatic weapons).

*A collapsible 8.8 cm gun on the* Kronprinz Wilhelm. *The cruiser* Karlsruhe *carried two of these for transfer and fitting aboard a liner at sea upon receipt of advice that she was to serve as an auxiliary cruiser. In the photograph training is being carried out under the eye of Leutnant zur See Biermann who was to lose his life in the sinking of the sailing vessel* Ecclipse *in her flight from internment in America.*

*Starboard forward torpedo tube and 15 cm aboard the* Wolf. *The muzzle of another gun within the fo'c's'le can just be seen in the angle between the side of the fo'c's'le and the barrel of the nearer gun. Part of the bulwark is hinged to drop downwards. The torpedo was brought to bear on the target by means of a form of gun-sight mounted along the top of its tube, the firing position being determined after taking into account the speed of the target ship.*

*The port forward 15 cm gun of the* Atlantis. *The photo shows clearly how their concealing shutters were opened.*

*Two 15 cm guns on the auxiliary cruiser* Widder. *Above the splinter protection, which these old casemate weapons had had built over them, can be seen as disguise mock-ups of cable-drums. The 'rammer' is lifting his ram to put a fresh shell and charge into the breech after the fall of the previous shot. Regular ramming keeps dispersal to a minimum so his job is an important one.*

**Left and below left** *These two photographs show the port 15 cm gun aboard* Michel, *the upper forward gun and the lower one next to it. The concealing shutters could be dropped quickly with their counter-weights to provide a clear arc of fire. To the left of the gun sits a man responsible for its correct elevation, and to the right would be the man responsible for its deflection. The gunnery officer's orders are received by telephone and repeated back. Behind the breech stand the gun-layers (ready to load) and the man ready to close it.*

**Below** *Practice shoot aboard the* Widder; *only the 15 cm guns are taking part. The gun in the foreground has just been fired and the barrel is still recoiled. Cordite smoke drifts across.*

**This page** These four photographs show different ways in which the 15 cm guns were camouflaged: on the foredeck as locomotive fireboxes, on the after hatch as carley floats, as a deckhouse on the poop and again as a deckhouse showing folding shutters. The lifeboat in the third picture is part of the disguise and would be lowered out of the way on the order 'drop camouflage'. The gun's muzzle can be seen just to the left of the ventilator. The ship is the Orion.

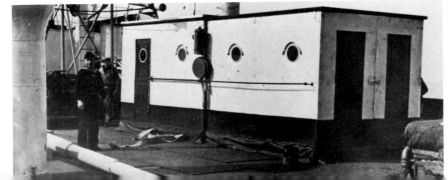

## Torpedoes

The *Normannia*'s only torpedo tubes were on her steam pinnaces. As the first of the second generation of auxiliary cruisers, the *Meteor* carried a single tube on each side forward of the bridge as close-range defensive weapons. They were fixed, so the *Meteor* herself had to manoeuvre in order to enable them to be sighted on the target. This was not the case with the *Möwe* and the *Wolf* (II), which had swivel-mounts. The commander of the *Orion*, which was the slowest of the Second World War auxiliary cruisers, asked for and received triple swivel-mounted torpedo tubes for his ship. Other auxiliary cruisers had fixed single or double tubes above the waterline. However, as a torpedo fired from one of these made a splash as it hit the water, thereby warning the attacked ship and giving her the opportunity of taking evasive action, additional torpedo mountings were later installed below the waterline (presumably at right angles to the ships' sides). Torpedo type G 7 was used throughout the

First World War and G 7a during the Second.

Each type could be set to run at a fast speed over a short distance or at a slower rate over a long stretch. For close-range action they could be regulated to a very high speed, proving themselves in this respect when used by the *Meteor* in her action against the British armed boarding vessel *The Ramsey*, and later in the destruction of the light cruiser HMAS *Sydney* by the *Kormoran*.

During the First World War, torpedoes exploded on direct contact with the hull of the target ship. This was also the case during the Second World War, but the more sophisticated type could be set optionally to travel beneath the target's hull, when its magnetic field would cause it to detonate.

**Torpedo strike in which the steamer *Empire March* was sunk by the auxiliary cruiser *Michel* and the fast motor launch *Esau* on January 2 1943**

|  | *Michel* Starboard above water | Port tubes | *Esau* Starboard after tubes | Port |
|---|---|---|---|---|
| Type of torpedo | G 7v | G7v | F 1 | F 2 |
| Torpedo speed in knots | 32 | 40 | 30 | 30 |
| Depth in metres at which set | 3 | 3 | 3 | 3 |
| Safety interval in metres | 300 | 150 | 150 | 150 |
| Range in metres | 3500 | 3500 | Max | Max |

*Sectional elevation of the* Möwe *showing her general arrangement. The commander and officers were accommodated adjacent to the bridge whence they could proceed to action stations quickly. The hospital was on the shelter deck where the wards would receive maximum daylight and fresh air. On each side of the engine casing a trackway led from the forward end of the mine deck aft. Ammunition was hoisted to the respective firing positions by the quickest routes. Part of each hold served as a coal bunker.*

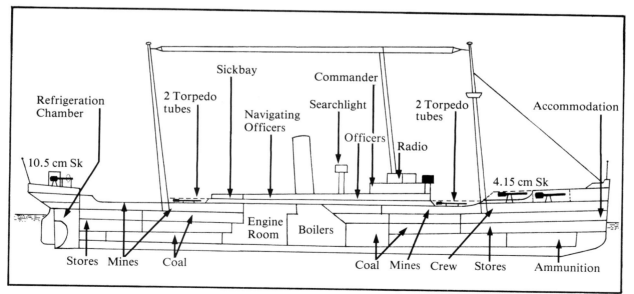

**Above** *Aboard the* Möwe *during her second cruise. A view taken from the bridge deck looking aft showing a life raft on the shelter deck, the after spare torpedo (in its 7 m casing by the bulwarks), the torpedo tube swivel mounting, the poop, dolly-winches and other fittings, emergency steering wheel and magnetic compass.*

**Above right** *A torpedo is fired from the* Widder. *Half of it has left the tube and still has its suspension stud in the T-shaped rebate of the projecting spoon of the tube. Not until the stud has cleared the end of the tube does the torpedo drop when it attains its ejection speed of 25 m per second.*

**Right** *The* Widder *fires a torpedo.*

## Mines

If one excepts the former express steamer *Berlin*, the first German auxiliary cruiser to be used for minelaying was the inconspicuous and typically British-looking *Meteor*. A mine laid by the *Berlin* achieved what was undoubtedly the greatest success in mine warfare against Great Britain, the sinking of the battleship HMS *Audacious*. Frantic mine-sweeping followed Great Britain's realisation that five merchant ships and one of her pre-'Dreadnought' battleships had been sunk through striking mines, all laid by the *Meteor* and the *Möwe*. The largest score was achieved by the *Wolf* (II) whose mines sank 13 cargo vessels totalling 75,688 GRT—and those are only the ones which actually foundered as a result of the damage they received. The *Orion's* mines sank six (24,118 GRT plus two trawlers), while those of the *Pinguin* and her auxiliary *Passat* (whose mines had come from the *Pinguin)* accounted for four (18,068 GRT).

### Particulars of the mines carried by auxiliary cruisers during the Second World War

|  | EMC | TMB II |
|---|---|---|
| Total weight | 1,135 kg | 740 kg |
| Weight of charge | 250 kg | 540 kg |
| Height overall | 1,940 mm | 560 mm |
| Length in the track | 1,235 mm | 2,306 mm |
| Safety interval (from mine to mine as laid) | 100 m | 130 m |

Maximum speed of a minelayer when laying mines from a height of:

|  | EMC | TMB II |
|---|---|---|
| 4.5 m | 25 kn | 22 kn |
| 5.0 m | 18 kn | 18 kn |

### Minelaying from auxiliary cruisers

EMC, electric mine, type C: contact with a lead horn broke an acid-filled glass tube. The acid flowed over a plate and caused detonation.

The EMC rested on a four-wheeled cradle which moved on a track. A fifth wheel guided the mine and cradle connection up to the point of severance when the mine cleared the ship. A weighted sinker on a line of predetermined length was connected to the mine and fixed it at a point below the surface of the water. A cable continued to link the mine with its cradle until the weighted sinker reached the sea bed, when the mine was freed.

### Laying from fast motor launches

TMB, type B: this could be carried in and laid from a torpedo tube, for example from a submerged submarine. It was a ground mine which detonated when a magnetic field was created between itself and a ship passing overhead. It was constructed to fit into a 53-cm torpedo tube.

Each type of mine could be set with a safety fuze of either 25 to 50 or ten to 30 minutes' duration.

Linked with minelaying was the sinking of intercepted ships with a minimum of outlay using explosive charges. Up to 50 kg of explosive could be used depending upon the size of the ship. It would be set to destroy the condenser outlet or inlet and let the sea pour in. The charge was detonated through a pre-set fuze.

**Below** *Minelaying scaffolding—here seen on the auxiliary minelayer* Bulgaria—*was fitted to auxiliary cruisers, within the hull and protected and concealed behind shutters.*

**Above** *The auxiliary cruiser Möwe—sailing as 'Auxiliary Steamer 10' (see the lettering on the funnel)—lies alongside the former train ferry* Deutschland *which is serving as a minelayer. Between the torpedo tube swivel mounting and the after hatch is the mine trackway consisting of two parallel U-section girders screwed into the deck. The track leads along the side alleyway to the level of the forward mine store whence the mines are loaded on the track.*

**Right** *An EMC-type mine on deck.*

**Right** *An EMC-type mine in mid-air. The axles with the four casters can be seen and the fifth wheel which acted as 'feeler'.*

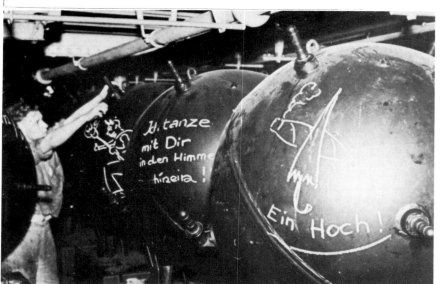

**Above** *The mine trackway on* Möwe. *In the foreground a piece of rail will be seen to have been removed so that mines from the after mine store can be guided on to the track. To the left protective plating covers the chains, rods and guide-pulleys which link the bridge steering position with the rudder.*

**Left** *EMC-type mines have their sensitive horns examined.*

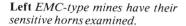

**Left** *Mines from the* Pinguin *are ferried across to the* Passat.

# Communications

By the outbreak of the First World War, signals and radio officers *(Signaloffizierer* and *Funktelegraphie-offizierer)* had been introduced as appointments aboard German auxiliary cruisers. The former were in charge of visual and the latter of W/T communications. Before the Second World War started, both appointments had been combined into that of *Bordnachrichtenoffizier* (communications officer). International Code of Signals flags continued to play their part in auxiliary cruiser communications with intercepted vessels but, apart from this, radio was driving ahead.

The only known photograph of an auxiliary cruiser's radio room—that of the *Michel*—is reproduced below. Pictures of D/F and coding equipment and rooms used by monitoring groups are not available, presumably because photographing them was so strictly forbidden.

Communications work meant keeping a watch on all radio traffic, not just that which directly affected one's own ship. Results were obtained from correct evaluation of apparently unimportant messages, and their correlation to other traffic. These could concern sinkings, captures or the avoidance of patrolling enemy cruisers.

Again and again a report from the radio room would affect a commander's decision, particularly when messages from a ship which had been stopped or ordered to stop were being monitored. The report 'Ship sending!' could be followed immediately by the order from the bridge 'Open fire!' Men's lives and the fate of a ship could depend on the accuracy of a report from the radio room.

The extent to which an irresponsible radio crew could negate the fortunes of an auxiliary cruiser was demonstrated in the case of the *Berlin.* Her commander decided to make for the neutral port of Trondheim after his radio room had reported that the British were waiting for him between Scotland and Norway. As he was soon to learn, however, the powerful units of the Grand Fleet said to be cruising in the North Sea existed only in the heads of his telegraphists.

*Inside the* Michel*'s radio room.*

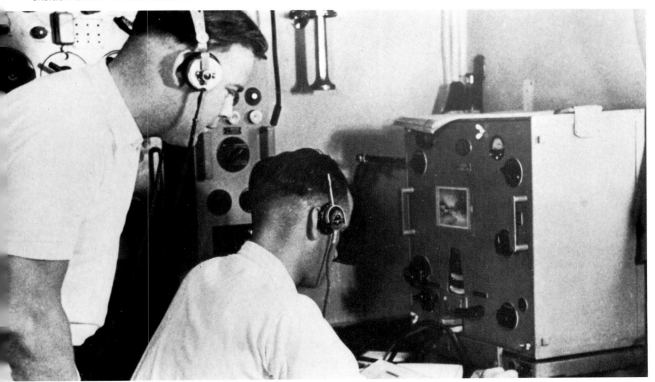

## Torpedo-carrying pinnaces

Both the old Imperial Navy and the later *Kriegs-marine* put into practice the idea that the effective-ness of auxiliary cruisers could be increased by equipping them with small torpedo boats in addition to the tubes they already had on board. So it was that in 1895 the *Normannia*, the German Navy's first auxiliary cruiser, carried two 'non-autonomous' torpedo boats. They were classed as 'non-autonomous' because they were not indepen-dent of the ship's command structure. Between about 1890 and 1900, steam pinnaces, each armed with a 45 cm torpedo tube, were among the small craft carried by both heavy and light units of the

Germany Navy. The cruiser *Irene* was one of them. Strictly speaking, the craft were no more than a means of improving the accuracy of torpedoes fired from a distance.

The idea caught on again in 1936 and the *Seekriegsleitung* accordingly asked for plans to be prepared for a high-speed torpedo-equipped launch which could be carried by cruisers and auxiliary cruisers for offensive use. The resulting tender was for a boat of wood and light metal construction 20 metres in length and armed with a bow torpedo tube, but it was turned down as being too heavy and hard to handle. Following clarification of the number of torpedoes and tubes to be carried as well as the method of firing, if was decided that two 45 cm tubes should be fitted astern but trained forward. A minimum speed of about 20 knots was asked for, taking into account the fact that the torpedoes already have a forward momentum when they enter the water. This arrangement was advan-tageous in that the target could be kept under observation throughout the period of actual firing. At the moment of ejection, however, the launch would have to increase her speed and turn ahead of the pursuing torpedo.

As the torpedo tubes were not ready in time, the first two light high speed motor launches (LS), numbers 2 and 3, designed to be carried by auxiliary cruisers, were respectively given instead three and four type TMB magnetic mines. Not until the commissioning of *LS 4* were twin torpedo tubes fitted as originally planned.

Specifications were as follows: light metal-framed V-section bottom from Dornier, Friedrichs-hafen; displacement 11.5 cu m, length 12.50 m, breadth 3.46 m, working draught 0.92 m, limit 0.77 m; propulsion—*LS 2* and *3* had two Junkers six-cylinder two-stroke JUMO 205 diesels of 700 and 850 hp each respectively; *LS 4* had two Daimler-Benz 12-cylinder V-type four-stroke type MB 507 diesels, each of 850 hp; all boats had Stöckicht wheel drive (twin screw, each three-bladed, diameter 0.48 m) and twin rudders; armament—*LS 2* had three mines abreast, *LS 3* four mines in pairs abreast and above each other; *LS 2* mounted one 6 cm gun aft which was subsequently fitted on the *Komet* and later the *Adjutant;* against aircraft, one MG 15 in a turret mounting; *LS 3* and *4* each had a 2 cm quick-firing cannon.

The following points are worthy of note: On June

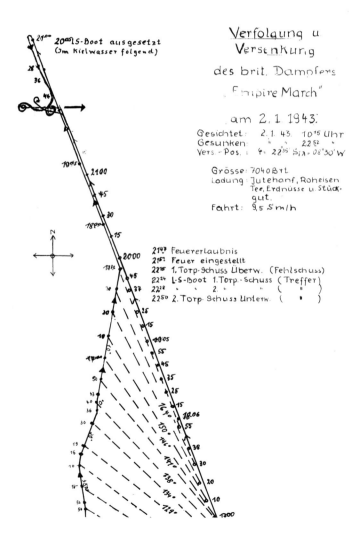

Verfolgung u Versenkung des brit. Dampfers „Empire March" am 2.1.1943.

Gesichtet: 2.1.43.  10¹⁵ Uhr
Gesunken:  „  „  22⁵²  „
Vers.-Pos.:  4: 22³⁵ S/n 08°30′W

Grösse: 7040 BrT
Ladung: Jutehanf, Roheisen Tee, Erdnüsse u. Stückgut.
Fahrt: 9,5 S'm/h

21⁴⁷ Feuererlaubnis
21⁵¹ Feuer eingestellt
22⁰⁵ 1.Torp.-Schuss Überw. (Fehlschuss)
22²⁴ L.S-Boot 1.Torp.-Schuss (Treffer)
22²⁸  „  „  2.  „  ( „ )
22⁵⁰ 2.Torp.-Schuss Unterw. ( „ )

Equipment for war

69

*One of the two Arado 231 planes carried by the* Stier.

*To replace her discarded Arado, in the early part of 1941 the* Orion *obtained in Japan a Nakajima 90-11 with centre floats. It was equipped with a Nakajima-Jupiter nine-cylinder radial engine of 450/500 hp. The aircraft was a biplane delivered tested and fitted with German armament and radio equipment. Top speed: 220 km/h, landing speed 80 km/h, flight endurance 6.3 hours.*

*One of* Atlantis' *two He 114b aircraft is prepared for take-off. It has been hoisted out of the hold and rests on the hatch cover. As a 'one and a half winger', the plane had a long upper and a short lower wing, the former constructed to fold back.*

## Analysis of auxiliary cruiser armament
### Guns

**Abbreviations used for the *Normannia* and First World War auxiliary cruisers**

| | |
|---|---|
| K 15 | = 15 cm gun L/ . . |
| SK 15/45 | = 15 cm SK L/45 |
| SK 15/40 | = 15 cm SK L/40 |
| K 12.5 | = 12.5 cm K L/ . . |
| SK 10.5 | = 10.5 cm SK L/40 |
| K 10.5 | = 10.5 cm K L/40 |
| K 9 | = 9 cm K L/ . . |
| SK 8.8/45 | = 8.8 cm SK L/45 |
| SK 8.8 zer | = 8.8 cm SK L/45 on collapsible mounting* |
| SK 8.8 L/40 | = 8.8 cm SK L/40 |
| SK 5.2 | = 5.2 cm SK L/55* |
| RK | = 3.7 cm swivel gun (as mounted on the *Normannia*'s 'non-autonomous' torpedo-boats) |
| MK | = 3.7 cm quick-firing cannon |

* For fitting aboard ships designated as future Naval auxiliaries and auxiliary cruisers; zer = zerlegbar (collapsible).

**Abbreviations used for Second World War auxiliary cruisers**

| | | *Range in metres* |
|---|---|---|
| TK 15 | = 15 cm torpedo boat gun L/48 | 17,000 |
| SK 15 | = 15 cm SK MPL adapted, with protection | 16,700 |
| Flak 10.5 | = 10.5 cm Flak L/45 | ca 15,000 |
| Flak 8.8 | = 8.8 cm Flak L/45 | ca 10,000 |
| SK 7.5 | = 7.5 cm SK L/35** | ca 8,000 |
| Bootsk | = 6 cm boat gun L/18** | ca 4,000 |
| Flak 4 | = 4 cm Flak Bofors | ca 10,000 |
| II 3.7 | = 3.7 cm SK C/30 (L/50) | ca 9,000 |
| PAK | = 3.7 cm anti-tank gun** | |
| II 2 | = 2 cm MK in twin mounting C/38 | ca 6,000 |
| I 2 | = 2 cm MK in single mounting (MGC/30) | ca 6,000 |

** Intended as 'stop' guns

MK = Large-calibre automatic weapon.

RK = Revolver gun, a group of five parallel barrels rotating on an intermediate axis.

Bootsk = A gun which can be used from a ship's boat or on land from a wheeled carriage.

MPL adapted = These were the guns from the pre-'Dreadnought' battleships *Schlesien* and *Schleswig-Holstein,* taken out of their casemates and fitted with armour protection for their crews and otherwise adapted.

Flak = Anti-aircraft gun.

SK = Quick-firing gun.

K = Gun (old type with low rate of fire).

L/ . . = Length of barrel in calibres.

C/ . . = Year of construction.

## Torpedo armament
### Torpedoes

The *Normannia*'s 'non-autonomous' torpedo boats carried weapons of 45 cm calibre. With the exception of the *Meteor* (45 cm), all First World War auxiliary cruisers carried torpedoes of 50 cm calibre. Those of the Second World War were of 53.3 cm. The fast motor launch *Esau* carried by the *Michel* fired 45 cm Type F 1 torpedoes. These were normally supplied to aircraft.

### Torpedo tubes

First World War auxiliary cruisers fired their torpedoes from fixed tubes. These would be mounted to point outboard but being then fixed in the one position, the ship herself would have to be swung in order to bring a target into line. With one exception this method held good for the above-water tubes of the Second World War auxiliary cruisers, and also where underwater tubes were fitted. The exception was the *Orion* which had two triple torpedo tube mountings that could be turned to the desired angle of fire. Her commander required this type because of this ship's low speed and the time she took to make the necessary turns.

### Abbreviations

I TR = single tube.

II TR = twin tube.

III TR = triple tube.

*übw* = above water, *untw* = underwater.

## The armament of individual auxiliary cruisers

*Numbers in brackets denote number of rounds of ammunition or torpedoes carried.*

*Normannia:* eight K 15s, four K 12.5s, two K 9s and six RKs; two 22-ton 'non-autonomous' torpedo boats, each with one I TR 45 cm (8).

*Kaiser Wilhelm der Große:* six SK 10.5s (400) and two MKs (200).

*Cormoran:* eight K 10.5s (1,200) from the 'unprotected' cruiser *Cormoran.*

*Prinz Eitel Friedrich:* four SK 10.5s (*ca* 900), six SK 8.8/40s and four MKs (9,000) from the gunboats *Luchs* and *Tiger.*

*Kronprinz Wilhelm:* two SK 8.8 *zer* (300) starboard forward supplied by the light cruiser *Karlsruhe* from the stock she carried to equip auxiliary cruisers. From October 8 1914: two 12 cm SKs from the *La Correntina* astern but no rounds for them.
*Cap Trafalgar:* two SK 10.5s (482) and four MKs (9,000) from the gunboat *Eber.*
*Berlin:* two SK 10.5s (300), one starboard forward and one port aft, six MKs (600) and 200 mines.
*Vineta:* four SK 15 L/40s (600) and four SK 8.8/45s.
*Meteor:* two SK 8.8 L/40s (600), two MKs and 347 mines. On her second cruise she carried in addition one SK 15 L/. . astern and two I TR 45s (2) *übw.*
*Möwe:* four SK 15 L/45s (600), one SK 10.5/45 (200) and two I TR 50s *übw* (12).*
*Wolf* (I): four SK 15 L/40s (600), two MKs and two I TR 50s *übw* (16).
*Greif:* four SK 15 L/40s (600), one SK 10.5 L/40 (200) and two I TR 50s *übw* (12).
*Wolf* (II): seven SK 15 L/40s (1,200), four I TR 50s (16), 465 mines, one Friedrichshafen E33 aircraft and three SK 5.2s (600) for supplying to other auxiliaries.
*Seeadler:* two SK 10.5 L/45s (400).
*Geier:* two SK 5.2s (300) from the auxiliary cruiser *Möwe.*
*Leopard:* five SK 15 L/40s (600), four SK 8.8 L/40s and two I TR 50s (12).
*Iltis:* one SK 5.2 (200) and 25 mines supplied by the *Wolf* (II).
*Orion:* six SK 15s (1,800), one SK 7.5, two II 3.7s (400), two II 2s (8,000), two III TRs *übw,* 228 EMC mines and one Ar 196A-1 (from February 1941, one Nakajima).

* 500 type E mines and two SK 5.2s (400) for equipping other naval auxiliaries.

*Atlantis:* six SK 15s (1,800), one SK 7.5, one II 3.7 (4,000), two II 2s (8,000), four I TRs *übw,* 92 EMC mines and two He 114Bs.
*Widder:* six SK 15s (1,800), one SK 7.5, two II 3.7s (4,000), two II 2s (8,000), two II TRs *übw* and two He 114Bs.
*Thor:* six SK 15s, from 1942 replaced by six TK 15s (1,800). Until 1942: one Bootsk, one II 3.7 (4,000), two II 2s (8,000), two II TRs *übw* and one Ar 196A-1.
*Pinguin:* six SK 15s (1,800), one SK 7.5, one II 3.7 (4,000), two II 2s (8,000), two II TRs *übw,* 300 EMC mines and two He 114Bs (from March 1941 one Ar 196A-1).
*Stier:* six TK 15s (1,800), one II 3.7 (4,000), two II 2s (8,000), two I TRs *untw* and two Ar 231s.
*Komet:* six SK 15s (1,500), one Bootsk and one II 3.7 (4,000). From 1942: two 3.7s, two II 2s (8,000), two II TRs *übw,* 30 EMC mines for motor launch, one Ar 196A-1 and one motor launch *(LS 2)* for minelaying.
*Kormoran:* six SK 15s (1,800), one SK 7.5 aboard only up to the time of her sailing; two PAKs (3,000), one II 3.7 (4,000), five I 2s (10,000), two II TRs *übw,* two I TRs *untw,* 360 EMC mines, 30 TMB mines for motor launch, two Ar 196A-1s and one motor launch *(LS 3)* for minelaying.
*Michel:* six SK 15s (1,800), one Flak 10.5 (400), two II 3.7s (8,000), two II 2s (8,000), two II TRs *übw,* two I TRs *untw,* two Ar 196A-3s, one motor launch *(LS 4),* two 45 cm torpedo tubes.
*Coronel:* six TK 15s (6,000), six Flak 4s (12,000), four II 2s (16,000); a few I 2s. Designed to carry three aircraft but these were not put aboard.
*Hansa:* eight TK 15s (960), one Flak 10.5 (200), four II 3.7s (9,000), 18 II 2s (56,000); from about the autumn of 1944 altogether 28 light Flak. Up to 1944: two I TRs *übw,* two I TRs *untw,* one aircraft catapult. No aircraft actually put aboard.

# Training

The training necessary for service aboard the mobilised express steamers of 1914 was elementary compared with that demanded for the cargo vessels which had been converted for offensive action. In the light of experience an increasingly high standard of training came to be demanded for the Second World War auxiliary cruisers. As in the First World War, most of this was undertaken in the Baltic.

**Below** *The ship's company of the* Michel *led by their officers on parade in Danzig in July 1941.*

**Right** *A well-nigh peaceful scene at Kiel in April 1940. The auxiliary cruisers* Thor *(left) and* Pinguin *are moored to their respective buoys. Further to the left are the gunnery training ship* Brummer *and the gantries of the Howaldtswerke shipyard. To the right are a pre-'Dreadnought' battleship, either the* Schlesien *or the* Schleswig-Holstein, *and the big floating dock of the Deutsche Werft yard. The photograph was taken from the* Widder.

# Operation orders

The communications officer of every ship designated for use as an auxiliary cruiser was supplied with an operation order. In the First World War this came from the *Admiralstab* and in the Second World War from the *Seekriegsleitung* or from the commanding officer of a raider to one of his officers who was to take command of an additional raider. The order would quote either Imperial authority or 'Instructions for commanders of naval vessels overseas in the event of war'. Each type of order set out the basic rules with which the officers were to comply. They covered the role to be played by his particular ship and included a review of the political situation, enemy dispositions, the military forces relevant to various theatres of operation and, in the light of these, directions for the implementation of his duties. The boundaries of operational areas *(Op Gebiet)* were also listed, with instructions for the attainment of objectives as well as guidelines for a war on commerce and information on sources of supply and intelligence material.

# Departure

The British Isles lie across the North Sea and in both world wars have formed a barrier commanding all Germany's maritime outlets to the rest of the world. In the north they combine with the chain of islands towards Greenland which, when in enemy hands, increased every German ship's chance of interception, capture or destruction. In both world wars German ships, outward or homeward bound, from humble trawlers to the great battleship *Bismarck,* had to contend with the line of cruisers, armed merchant cruisers, aircraft carriers and other ever-watchful craft which were stretched between these islands. Breaking through this line was of primary importance but was also the hardest of problems, for nowhere else on the high seas were such dangers to be encountered. However, the map and survey opposite show that once an auxiliary cruiser succeeded in breaking through this cordon, she had to be taken as seriously as any regular naval unit, with the possible exception of the U-boat. Both outward and homeward voyages had to be carefully scheduled.

During the Second World War the position changed at a stroke with the occupation of the northern and western coasts of France. The weight of air attacks on French ports, coupled with the measures taken to prevent the auxiliary cruisers reaching the oceans either through the English Channel or the North Sea, demonstrated clearly that the Allies appreciated their significance. Nothing seemed to be too much trouble to take against the dreaded raiders. Agents were planted in ports and, during the First World War, their activities helped to seal the fate of the auxiliary cruiser *Greif,* one which would similarly have overtaken the *Wolf* (I) had she not stranded in the Elbe. It would seem, too, that the departure time of the *Komet*'s second cruise was known to the enemy beforehand, so that her break-out was intercepted, while the *Coronel* was attacked and forced to put back.

It is therefore clear why commanders should have chosen the most remote yet least dangerous route: the Denmark Strait between Greenland and Iceland. However, the time of year and constriction of sea lanes by ice were considerations which a commander had to take into account both before setting out on and during a cruise. These are made clear in the facsimile of part of the *Pinguin*'s log shown on page 76.

Mention should also be made of the *Komet*'s northern voyage and of auxiliary cruiser landfalls and departures in Japan.

*Heavy weather in the North Atlantic* (Orion).

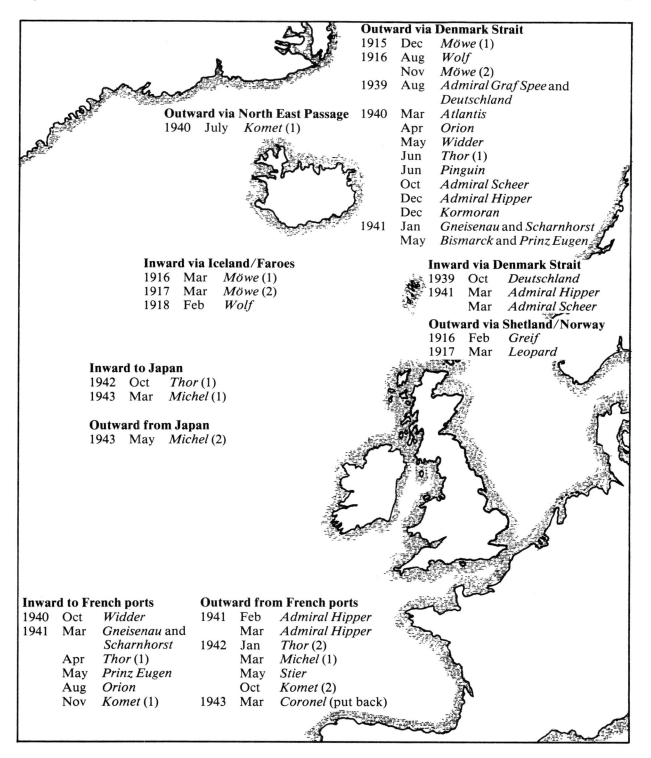

**Outward via Denmark Strait**

| 1915 | Dec | *Möwe* (1) |
|---|---|---|
| 1916 | Aug | *Wolf* |
| | Nov | *Möwe* (2) |
| 1939 | Aug | *Admiral Graf Spee* and *Deutschland* |
| 1940 | Mar | *Atlantis* |
| | Apr | *Orion* |
| | May | *Widder* |
| | Jun | *Thor* (1) |
| | Jun | *Pinguin* |
| | Oct | *Admiral Scheer* |
| | Dec | *Admiral Hipper* |
| | Dec | *Kormoran* |
| 1941 | Jan | *Gneisenau* and *Scharnhorst* |
| | May | *Bismarck* and *Prinz Eugen* |

**Outward via North East Passage**

| 1940 | July | *Komet* (1) |
|---|---|---|

**Inward via Iceland/Faroes**

| 1916 | Mar | *Möwe* (1) |
|---|---|---|
| 1917 | Mar | *Möwe* (2) |
| 1918 | Feb | *Wolf* |

**Inward via Denmark Strait**

| 1939 | Oct | *Deutschland* |
|---|---|---|
| 1941 | Mar | *Admiral Hipper* |
| | Mar | *Admiral Scheer* |

**Outward via Shetland/Norway**

| 1916 | Feb | *Greif* |
|---|---|---|
| 1917 | Mar | *Leopard* |

**Inward to Japan**

| 1942 | Oct | *Thor* (1) |
|---|---|---|
| 1943 | Mar | *Michel* (1) |

**Outward from Japan**

| 1943 | May | *Michel* (2) |
|---|---|---|

**Inward to French ports**

| 1940 | Oct | *Widder* |
|---|---|---|
| 1941 | Mar | *Gneisenau* and *Scharnhorst* |
| | Apr | *Thor* (1) |
| | May | *Prinz Eugen* |
| | Aug | *Orion* |
| | Nov | *Komet* (1) |

**Outward from French ports**

| 1941 | Feb | *Admiral Hipper* |
|---|---|---|
| | Mar | *Admiral Hipper* |
| 1942 | Jan | *Thor* (2) |
| | Mar | *Michel* (1) |
| | May | *Stier* |
| | Oct | *Komet* (2) |
| 1943 | Mar | *Coronel* (put back) |

```
                                    - 16 -
┌────────┬────────────────────────┬──────────────────────────────────────────┐
│ Datum  │ Angabe des Ortes, Wind,│              Vorkommnisse                  │
│ und    │ Wetter, Seegang, Be-   │                                            │
│ Uhrzeit│ leuchtung, Sichtigkeit │                                            │
│        │ der Luft, Monbschein   │                                            │
│        │ usw.                   │                                            │
├────────┼────────────────────────┼────────────────────────────────────────────┤
│ 29.6.  │ OzN 6                  │ Der erwartete Warmlufteinbruch ist einge-   │
│ 0600ʰ  │ Seegang 4,D 2          │ treten. In sehr diesigem Wetter wird der    │
│        │ bedeckt,Regen,neblig   │ Vormarsch bei starkem Regen in die          │
│        │                        │ Dänemarkstrasse angetreten.                 │
│ 1547ʰ  │ ONO 6                  │ Kurz nach Passieren der eigentlichen Enge   │
│        │ Seegang 5,D 3          │ kommen einzelne Eisschollen, später häufiger│
│        │ neblig,schlechte Sicht │ werdende,grössere Eisblöcke im Dunst in     │
│        │                        │ Sicht, denen ausgewichen werden muss.       │
```

Schliesslich ist ein Ausweichen nicht mehr möglich,es wird nun energisch von der Eisgrenze abgedreht,um wieder freies Wasser zu erreichen.

Zum Durchbruch durch die Dänemarkstraße ist abschließend zu bemerken:

Der Durchbruch erscheint im Sommer - also ohne Dunkelwerden - möglich, wenn genügend Zeit verfügbar ist, eine für den Durchbruch günstige Wetterlage abzuwarten. Die Wartestellung sollte stets in Nebelgebieten liegen bzw. soweit von Island abgesetzt sein, daß eine Erfassung durch eine mögliche Luftaufklärung von Island aus unwahrscheinlich ist.

Als für einen Durchbruch günstig ist entweder das Passieren eines entgegenkommenden Tiefs in der Dänemarkenge oder eine Wetterlage anzusehen, die von Süden größere Mengen Warmluft bis nördlich Island heraufbringt. Letztere Wetterlage wurde von Schiff 33 für den Durchbruch ausgenutzt.

Selbst eine stärkere Bewachung der Dänemarkstraße als bisher, etwa mit Fischdampfern und Hilfskreuzern, läßt unter den erwähnten Umständen im Sommer Durchbrüche möglich erscheinen.

Irgendeine Rückwirkung des Zusammentreffens mit dem englischen U-Boot bei der Ausfahrt aus dem Froisjöenfjord war während des Durchbruchs nicht zu bemerken.

Falls das U-Boot das Auslaufen des verdächtigen Dampfers als das eines Hilfskreuzers angesprochen und gemeldet hat, wird jetzt, nach erfolgtem Durchbruch des Schiffes in den Atlantik, das Wissen des Gegners um das Auslaufen eines weiteren Handelsstörers als im Sinne der Aufgabe des Schiffes liegend angesehen.

*Krüder*

**Facsimile of extract from *Pinguin*'s log**

29.6, 0600 hours: *E by N 6, Sea 4, D 2, obscured, rain hazy: The expected warm air stream has set in. The passage through the Denmark Strait has begun in very misty weather with heavy rain.*

*1547 hours: ENE 6, Sea 5, D 3: Shortly after the passage through the main strait there have been isolated ice floes, later, frequently occurring larger ice-blocks appearing through the mist which have to be avoided.*

*Eventually avoiding action is no longer possible and we push through the last stretches of ice to reach open water again.*

*To break through the Denmark Strait it is essential to note:*

*The breakthrough appears possible in summer when there is little darkness. If time is available, suitable weather should be awaited. The waiting place should invariably be in a foggy area as distant as possible from Iceland to avoid the possibility of being sighted from the aircraft based there.*

*For a successful breakthrough there should be either deep water in the Strait or a situation which brings low air pressure from the south to north of Iceland.*

*For her breakthrough Ship 33 has made use of the latter.*

*Apart from a stronger patrol on the Denmark Strait than hitherto, mainly armed trawlers and auxiliary cruisers, it appears under the above-mentioned circumstances that breakthroughs are possible in summer.*

*There was no reaction from a British submarine met during our departure from Froisjöenfjord.*

*Should the submarine have reported the sailing of a suspicious-looking ship as possibly that of an auxiliary cruiser, we shall have to take into account enemy knowledge of the existence at sea of yet another commerce destroyer.*

Krüder

# Routine

Once the auxiliary cruiser had broken through to the comparative freedom of the open sea and left behind some of the tension, the daily routine would begin, interrupted only when the occasional ship or aircraft was sighted. Watches were kept, as on other ships, on the bridge, in the engine and radio rooms, the hospital, and even in the bakery. Fighting efficiency was maintained by means of a training programme which was adhered to as far as circumstances allowed. Frequent practices or aircraft alarms were held when the crew would hasten to stations. The 'silent alarm' was also practised, when stations would be taken up quickly but in such a way as to be invisible from outboard. The ship's disguise would be maintained while further orders were awaited.

When the opportunity occurred, instructions in weapons and equipment and study of training manuals would be broken by sports. There were also opportunities for further education in such subjects as first aid and meteorology, as well as time for the pursuit of hobbies.

So life would go on. At dawn and dusk the commander and his officers would 'shoot' the stars or take a mid-day sight in order to calculate the ship's position. The officer of the watch would be

*Officers on the bridge of the* Möwe. *Leutnant zur See Meisel, adjutant and torpedo officer, is officer of the watch. One of his appointments during the Second World War was as commander of the heavy cruiser* Admiral Hipper.

responsible for keeping an eye on the lookout and helmsman, and be ready with the engine room telegraph. Down below, the engine room crew would stand four hours on and four off, complying with telegraphed orders from the bridge, supervising general running of the engines and fuel consumption. They would see also that the ship's auxiliary services were kept supplied with power, heat and water.

Potatoes would be taken out of store and peeled. In the ship's hospital all would be quiet, while the dental officer would use the time for an uninterrupted inspection of the teeth of everyone on board.

Depending upon the work-load, a few improvements would be made to the living quarters. The ship's safety in every conceivable eventuality was of particular concern. This floating community, for such did ship and crew together form, had to be prepared for whatever it might meet in its assigned area of operation.

The voyage thereto could take up to a few weeks and, provided it was free from incident, the crew could, so to speak 'shake down' into a team and get to know each other before the business of war began in earnest.

One ruse to deceive the enemy was a simulated

**Left** *A facsimile of the first page of a ship's newspaper, that of the Widder.*

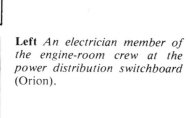

**Left** *An electrician member of the engine-room crew at the power distribution switchboard (Orion).*

**Right** *Keeping watch in the Orion's engine-room.*

radio conversation with an imaginary auxiliary cruiser not far away, to give any eavesdropper the impression that a large force of raiders might be in the vicinity, and possibly to indicate that one of them had a speed of around 25 knots. All these measures had the blessing of the *Seekriegsleitung* as 'related to the job in hand'.

Under these and similar circumstances the *Prinz Eitel Friedrich* cruised in the Pacific and the *Komet* fought her way through the Siberian ice-fields, while the *Orion*, making her bare 12 knots, almost literally crawled around Cape Horn and into the Pacific—only too aware that she could be spotted any minute.

**Right** *The* Obersteuermann *works at his charts while the look-out is at his post on the bridge* (Widder).

**Below right** *At the controls of the* Orion's *turbines. The engineer officer on watch will wear out his best uniform!*

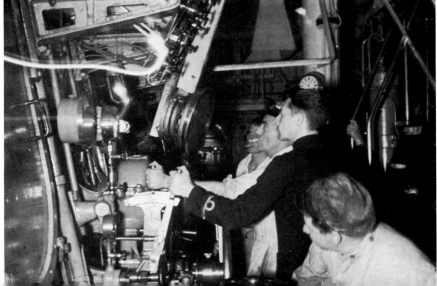

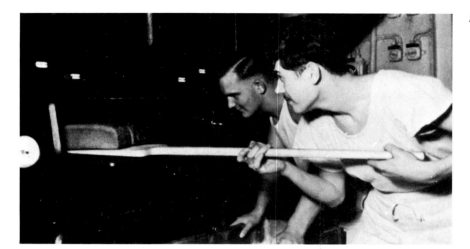

*Sailors as bakers* (Michel).

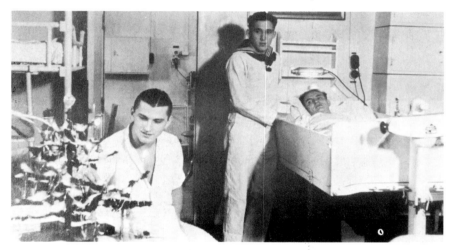

*Christmas in the ship's hospital, disrespectfully known to sailors as the* Schlunz, *a word translatable into English as 'the dump'* (Michel).

*The ship's lairage. Fresh meat is important for a crew's health.* (Widder).

**Above** . . . *And no mermaid to watch him!*

**Above right and right** *While two keep lookout from truck and crosstrees their off-watch ship-mates romp in the canvas-rigged swimming-pool.*

# The use of aircraft

In both world wars the aircraft carried by auxiliary cruisers were used mainly for reconnaissance and protection, in only a few instances for attack. Between the *Wölfchen* and the Arado 196/231s and Heinkels lay 25 years of development, so the aircraft of the Second World War were a far cry from the 'sticks and string' of the pioneers. Success was born of lessons learned from earlier mistakes.

Reconnaissance was based on a sort of dead-reckoning. Ceiling and flightpath were plotted to enable an aircraft to find its way back to the ship. On sighting a possible target it would either radio its report or return to the auxiliary cruiser with it. Frequently the aircraft would be ordered to maintain contact with the target so that the cruiser could plan her moves accordingly. Sometimes the aircraft would drop a bag containing orders steering the victim towards the cruiser. If she tried to make off, a bomb or two or a burst of machine-gun fire would reinforce the instruction.

A few pilots developed ideas of their own. One was to trail a weighted length of wire from the aircraft. This would be swept over and between the ship's masts, ripping away her radio aerial and so silencing any attempt to summon assistance.

Reconnaissance of islands or stretches of coastline was comparatively simple. It was not only easier but safer. If an aircraft's prolonged absence was causing anxiety aboard the parent auxiliary cruiser, a radio beam could be emitted on which a plane having navigational problems could 'home'.

One of an auxiliary cruiser's main concerns was to avoid being caught by surprise, and her aircraft helped prevent this by extending her range of vigilance. The fact that these protective flights were also instrumental in bringing in prizes demonstrated the co-operation between ship and aircraft as well as the versatility of each. During the Second World War, pilots aboard auxiliary cruisers were supplied by the German Navy.

The extent to which auxiliary cruisers were equipped to deal with every imaginable job through their workshops, stores and, above all, experienced personnel, is apparent from the instance cited in the caption opposite, where an entire aircraft engine frame was manufactured from scratch aboard the *Orion*.

Each Japanese aircraft carried by an auxiliary cruiser was fitted with a submersible rudder so that it could be steered like a ship while taxiing. German armament and equipment were built into these machines. The one involved in the incident depicted opposite had actually been paid for with part of a cargo of petrol from a tanker captured and taken to Japan.

*This Arado was badly damaged when landing on rough water. The incident happened on August 1 1940 and getting it back on board took a lot of effort* (Orion).

*This picture was taken from the Orion's aircraft. The subject speaks for itself.*

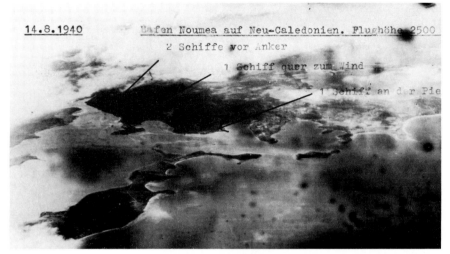

14.8.1940    Hafen Noumea auf Neu-Caledonien. Flughöhe 2500
2 Schiffe vor Anker
1 Schiff quer zum Wind
1 Schiff an der Pie

*Landing after another mission the engine of Orion's Arado dropped off into the sea, taking with it the frame. The ship carried a spare engine but no frame, so one was welded up on board.*

*A sailor working on an Arado 196. The cockpit cover is folded back (Orion).*

**Left** *The Arado 231 is swung out of the* Stier's *hold and overboard prior to take-off.*

**Below** *The Arado's engine is started up as soon as the plane has been hoisted level with the bulwark so that it will have steerage way the moment it becomes water-borne, using its rudder.*

# Minelaying

At first the only auxiliary cruisers entrusted with minelaying were the *Berlin* and *Meteor*, but they performed with such skill as to put this type of auxiliary cruiser operation into a class of its own. At the beginning of her first patrol, before devoting herself exclusively to commerce raiding, the *Möwe* laid mines off the Gironde estuary in France. Similarly, the first orders to *Wolf* (II) were to mine the most important British Empire harbours and their approach channels within the Indian Ocean.

Colombo, Karachi, Calcutta and other points were on the *Admiralstab*'s target list, as were Cape Town, the Cape of Good Hope and the off-lying Agulhas Bank. The exigencies of war caused the *Wolf*'s commander to amend part of his orders and sow mines off the south-east coast of Australia and around New Zealand. His decision was justified as these mines achieved far greater results than those

laid by other auxiliary cruisers during the First World War. Either her commander had been selected for his skill in this type of operation or he had an expert on board with him.

Mines were not just dropped into the shipping lanes. Laying them called for skill and judgement. The direction and amount of traffic, its course and destination, the strength and direction of currents, tidal differences and the size-range of the ships against which the mines were aimed, were all

*The British battleship HMS* Audacious, *the largest and strategically most important victim of auxiliary cruiser minelaying operations. 27,000 tons, 22 kts, ten 13.5-in (34.4 cm) and 16 4-in (10.2 cm) guns. Served from October 16 1913 to October 27 1914 when she was lost, only 12 weeks after Britain had declared war on Germany.*

factors which had to be noted. Because of the danger of premature explosion through accidental contact between them, the mines had to be laid a reasonable distance apart and diagonally across the anticipated course of the target ships. During the actual laying, the mining vessel was forced to take an erratic course which could attract the suspicions of an observant watcher. An anchored mine would be moved by the tide, the taut mooring cable becoming diagonal to the surface instead of at right angles, when the mine itself would be then positioned at a greater depth than when first sown. For this reason ground mines were considered more reliable. Minefields had to be made as difficult as possible for the enemy to sweep once they were discovered through the loss of a ship. To this end, circumstances permitting, the mines would be laid in crevices on the sea bed.

The mines had to be laid neither too thickly nor too widely spaced. There had to be a split-second correlation between distance and timing. If the speed of the minelayer had to be altered for any reason, so had the time interval between each sowing.

The *Pinguin* was commanded by Ernst-Felix Krüder. He was experienced in mining and one of his most interesting tasks in October 1940 was fitting out the captured Norwegian tanker *Storstad* (8,998 GRT) as a minelayer to be renamed *Passat*. His log included the following entry for October 8:
*'As the ship is a tanker and therefore not likely to arouse suspicion I intend to use her in the role of auxiliary minelayer. On inspection, two rooms on the after superstructure flanking the engine-room trunk, with a track leading from each, will, after the clearance of their contents and with suitable disguise, provide inconspicuous storage for about 100 mines.'*

Detailed instructions as to how this was to be accomplished followed, together with the appointment of Leutnant zur See (reserve) Warning as commander with the acting rank of Kapitän-Leutnant, the mustering of a crew, and so on. A description of the ship's task was included: to lay mines off the Banks Strait and off the eastern and western entrances to the Bass Strait. For this purpose 110 mines were to be taken aboard.

Work proceeded during the night but not as smoothly as planned because the bathroom fittings in the two rooms proved difficult to remove. However, the next morning the first mine was floated across to the *Passat*, but proved a time-consuming operation. The next attempt, using a motor launch, did not take so long.

*'October 9 1940: 33 mines carried across by the time darkness fell. During the night further work was undertaken on camouflaging the mine-storage rooms in the superstructure.*

*'October 10 1940: Fitting out and equipping the* Passat. *The transfer of the mines was resumed at daybreak—in a continuous shuttle-service 110 mines had been transferred by 1430 hours. The last mine was decorated with a flag and the following poem:*

*'The* Storstad's *got her mines*
*She made us busy bees.*
*The sailors and the sorters*
*Were nearly on their knees.*
*They all deserve some medals*
*For how they've fought and won.*
*With 'slack!' and 'heave!' and elbow grease*
*The last mine's made its run.*
*Our dear Lieutenant Schmidt\**
*Has told us that's the lot,*
*So now the Homeland wants us*
*To give of all we've got.*
*Our shells must let the Tommy know*
*'All seas' the German hand,*
*His throat to cut as gaily we*
*Behind the Führer stand.*
*The Indian Ocean's now our sphere:*
*So, Tommy, do watch out!*

*'Pinguin'*

Indian Ocean, October 10 1940
Authors: Matrose Gefreiter Kehrein, Matrose H. Gefreiter Weber.

*'The working party, particularly the welders and carpenters, put up an excellent performance, day and night. As the last group left the* Passat *at 1800 hours, the England Song† was sung . . .*

*'October 12 1940, 0030 hours (15° 18' south, 109° 14' east):* Passat *dismissed. 'Ship 33' resumes her course towards the Sunda Strait—Australia, which has made us a present of this tasty morsel.'*

(\*Oberleutnant Schmidt was the *Passat*'s minelaying officer.)
(†'*Wenn wir fahren gegen England*'—'When we sail against England'.)

The auxiliary cruiser Geier *was converted from the French cargo steamer* Saint Theodore *captured by the* Möwe *during her second cruise. She was sunk by the* Möwe *with explosive charges after her machinery had become worn out following her successful sortie as a surface raider, on February 14 1917.*

*The auxiliary minelayer* Adjutant *was formerly the whale catcher* Pol IX, *one of those captured by the* Pinguin. *She was first attached to the* Pinguin, *then to the* Komet *and sent to mine the waters off New Zealand. Her work ended, she was used by the* Komet *for target practice and sunk on July 1 1941.*

*The* Pinguin's *motor launch takes a mine across to the* Storstad. *Altogether 110 mines were transferred in this way.*

*A mine being hoisted aboard the* Storstad. *How this Norwegian tanker was converted into an auxiliary minelayer is related in detail on the facing page.*

# The cruiser war

At last the auxiliary cruiser takes up station—the hunt is on!

Unless a possible prize had already advertised her whereabouts with her radio traffic the crew would have to wait for a call like this from the lookout: 'Smoke to starboard, 285 degrees'. The source of the smoke would rise slowly above the horizon. Recognition features would be flashed to the commander: number and type of masts and their disposition in relation to the funnel, then the superstructure and colour scheme. The bearing and distance would be shouted to the chartroom every ten minutes. Soon it would be possible to estimate the vessel's course and speed. Her size, type and nationality would be judged in the light of observers' experience, and all would pray that she would not turn out to be an enemy armed merchant cruiser, or a passenger liner. Satisfied on these points, the auxiliary cruiser's commander would decide to intercept. Trying not to look as though he intended it, he would alter course so as to close up with his victim, preferably somewhat astern so that the gun on the other ship's poop could be kept within range, a lesson learned from past experience.

At the calculated moment would come the order: 'Silent alarm!' The crew would hasten to action stations, preparing everything except actually dropping their ship's disguise. Only a few men would be visible about her decks, no more than would be expected on a ship of the raider's size under peacetime conditions. With a report over the intercom that she was altering course would come the order: 'Prepare for action!'

With: 'Hoist colours, drop disguise', the naval ensign would be run up, clearly recognisable, and the concealing flaps dropped to give the guns a clear field of fire. A shot across the bows would accompany the signal 'Heave-to at once!' Provided that all went according to plan and she did not attempt to use her radio, the intercepted ship would reply with her siren or loud-hailer. Three short blasts on the former would indicate that her engines were running astern to take the way off her and bring her to a complete stop.

She would then be ordered to send a boat across with her papers for examination in accordance with the Prize Ordinance. Next, the raider's commander would have to decide whether to release her, sink her, or send her back to Germany as a prize of war.

Such was the comparatively peaceful business of the early cruiser war, although it was practically to disappear in the latter half of the First World War. A favourite trick developed was for the captain of an intercepted vessel to adopt delaying tactics to gain time for an attempt at flight, such as claiming that the sea was too rough for him to order a boat across. With this the raider would send over one of her own with a boarding party, while the captain would probably continue to put all sorts of difficulties in the way. Guards would then be posted at key points, bringing the captured ship under control, if necessary by threat of armed force.

The results of the boarding party's search would be communicated to the raider's commander by signal lamp and he would then make his decision. If he opted to sink the ship he had to decide whether to put her crew into their boats with provisions sufficient to take them to the nearest land, or to bring them aboard his own vessel. If he decided to take the ship back to Germany he would have to supply a prize crew, mostly drawn from the boarding party and in many cases assisted by members of the ship's own crew.

The photographs on pages 92 to 96 illustrate vividly the bitter confrontations which took place between raiders and their victims. Cargo ships were increasingly being armed and radio operators becoming more and more ready to tap out the news that their ships were under attack, even though these measures were against the accepted rules of war. The worst example of abuse was for a ship to request medical assistance for her wounded and then to re-open fire with her stern gun. The scheme devised by the British for destroying U-boats during the First World War was also revived. The crew of an attacked ship would simulate a panic-abandonment in one or two boats, leaving behind a hidden gun crew. When the raider came into a suitable position she would receive a hail of shells. Nevertheless there was only one instance of a

*'Silent alarm'. Unseen from outboard, the crew rush to action stations* (Widder).

*The* Orion *hoists her battle flag as she intercepts her first victim, the* Tropic Sea, *on June 19 1940.*

*The* Orion*'s order to stop at once is clear and unmistakeable.*

*The* Widder*'s collapsible bulwarks are released to give her guns a clear arc of fire.*

*This picture gives a good idea of the details of the collapsible bulwarks* (Widder).

*The gun is clear of camouflage. Originally the* Widder *only had a plain protective casing. The additions were made shortly before she sailed on active service. The gun is ready for firing and directed towards its target.*

*The breech of a 15 cm gun. Ammunition lies ready, charges to the right of the gun, shells further to the left. The photograph would seem to have been taken during a practice shoot* (Widder).

raider's gun crew failing to overcome opposition in a very short time and gain control of her adversary.

Whether a victim was sunk, taken along as an auxiliary to supply other auxiliary cruisers, or sent back to Germany as a prize, would depend upon where the interception took place, the level of the ship's bunkers, her cargo and the immediate requirements of the raider herself. During the Second World War, captured vessels were frequently sent to Japan. Every opportunity of replenishing stores from a captured vessel was normally taken, a point emphasised by the commander of the *Orion* in his log when he deplored the over-hasty sinking of a ship by the *Komet,* with which he had been operating in partnership. Apparently the commander of the *Komet,* with his up-to-date vessel, did not appreciate the *Orion*'s continuing need, with her out-dated machinery, for the necessities of life; nor how her stocks of timber, sheet metal, paint and, above all, oxygen, had been run down. Every change in disguise required oxygen for metal cutting and welding. As far as possible fresh provisions were transferred from captured vessels in their entirety. Oil and water were pumped across subject to preliminary tests having proved satisfactory.

With the increasing severity of the respective U-boat campaigns in both world wars, strict compliance with the 'War on Commerce Prize Ordinance' went by the board. If it had not, all the auxiliary cruisers would in time have been sunk. As already noted, intercepted merchantmen could turn out to be heavily armed, and more and more did they radio reports when danger threatened. It was no longer sufficient simply to jam their broadcasts; shells had to be fired into their radio rooms. Until merchant ships began to be fitted with radar, an auxiliary cruiser could stalk his quarry by day and come up with him during the night. The aim was to achieve surprise, for a ship observed in daylight could become suspicious and escape under cover of darkness. Generally the raider was able to close with his victim quickly and take him unawares.

It goes without saying that an auxiliary cruiser's aircraft played an important part. Patrol range could be doubled from the usual 40 nautical miles with the help of German supply ships and captured enemy vessels as such ships could relay visual signals between two cruisers.

Despite the increasing bitterness of the fighting, humanity could not be forgotten. Unfortunately, as noted elsewhere, an alleged lack of this quality was used as an excuse for bringing von Ruckteschell before a British military court. He had commanded the *Widder* and *Michel* in succession and was accused of having fired upon the crew of a sinking ship as they were rowing away from her. His defence was that the boat, invisible in the darkness, was in the firing line as the *Davisian* was being shelled and sunk after she had been abandoned. There were no wounded in it.

The extent to which von Ruckteschell was unjustifiably victimised is indicated in this extract from his log written at the time of the *Empire*

*The* Widder*'s stern gun is cleared of camouflage and prepared for firing.*

*March*'s sinking on December 27 1942. The raider's aircraft had spotted the ship during the daylight reconnaissance. The fast motor launch *Esau* was despatched that night to mount an attack. The log describes what happened after the ship had been sunk by two torpedoes, one from the *Michel* and one from the *Esau:*

'*I recalled the launch. She had on board three prisoners taken in the course of the fighting. They were transferred to the* Michel. *In the meantime the launch received orders to look for and pick up any further survivors before being hoisted back on board. The* Michel *also used the time to rescue survivors, the first officer directing operations.*

'*2342 hours: The launch returned with 11 more prisoners, five of them badly injured. Between then and 0100 hours, more survivors were rescued from the water. The course over which the fighting had extended was retraced and boats and rafts examined. The crew numbered 58, of whom 25 have been rescued including the master, who is the only surviving officer. We have spent nearly two and a half hours on the rescue operations and intend to return to the scene of the sinking to-morrow to clear the area.*'

These extracts from the *Michel*'s log speak for themselves.

**Left** *The* Orion *emphasises with a warning shot her order to the* Tropic Sea *to stop.*

**Below** *The auxiliary cruiser* Widder *has despatched a boat with a search party to the British steamer* Davisian *(6,433 GRT) and they have climbed aboard. The* Davisian*'s crew have already launched one of their own boats and another is lowered to bridge deck level ready to be entered.*

**Right** *The British cargo vessel* Benavon *has tried to hit back, has been hit herself in several places and is ablaze practically from end to end.*

**Below** *The search party on the burning* Kemmendine *looks for any secret material which may have been left behind in the panic abandonment.*

PASSENGERS NOT ALLOWED FORWARD OF THIS RAIL

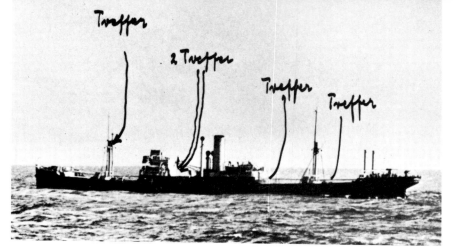

**Left** *A supplement to the* Thor*'s log: a photograph marked to show hits on the British steamer* Wendover *(5,489 GRT). She was sunk on July 16 1940.*

**Left** *The crew of a sunken ship pull alongside the* Atlantis.

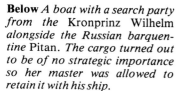

**Below** *A boat with a search party from the* Kronprinz Wilhelm *alongside the Russian barquentine* Pitan. *The cargo turned out to be of no strategic importance so her master was allowed to retain it with his ship.*

**Right** *Shortage of ammunition caused the* Kronprinz Wilhelm *to resort to having to ram the British schooner* Wilfred M, *but the timber cargo kept her afloat.*

**Right** *A picture which could have been taken during the First World War. The auxiliary cruiser* Widder *intercepts the Finnish barque* Killoran *and in sinking her makes her the only sailing vessel to have been destroyed by an auxiliary cruiser during the Second World War (August 10 1940, before Finland became allied to Germany).*

**Below** *The* Atlantis' *last sinking: the British steamer* Balzac *(5,372 GRT) under attack on June 22 1941.*

**Left** *The* Atlantis' *guns have had to be used more forcefully to persuade the master of the Norwegian* Talleyrand *to give in on August 2 1940.*

**Above** *This picture shows the effect of hits on the British tanker* Athelking. *Bridge, radio room and stern gun were always the most important targets on an intercepted ship which refused to stop and attempted to return fire.* Atlantis, *September 9 1940.*

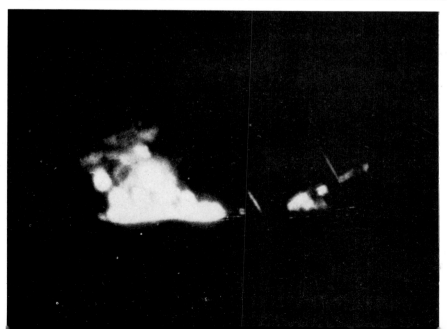

**Left** *The spectacular end of the Norwegian tanker* Beaulieu, *sunk on August 4 1940* (Widder).

# Hunting the whalers

The honour of securing the biggest prize in the shortest time goes to the auxiliary cruiser *Pinguin* which, between January 13 and 15 1941, captured two Norwegian Antarctic whaling fleets. This account is less concerned with the events of those three days than with the manner of their accomplishment. No one has described their sequence more clearly and forcibly than the *Pinguin*'s commander in his log, from which three facsimile extracts are reproduced on the next two pages. Twenty-eight hours elapse between the first and second extract, during which time the decision was taken to go ahead with the operation, and 22 hours elapse between the second and third. Less important passages have been omitted and, in the second and third extracts, the second columns with their notes on the weather, etc.

The *Pinguin* had been quietly monitoring the whalers' radio traffic so that their habits and the nature of their conversation had become familiar to her. She was also able to gain some idea of what the various ships looked like and had identified the factory ship *Ole Wegger* (12,201 GRT) and *Pelagos* (12,083 GRT), and the depot ship *Solglimt* (12,246 GRT) which was due to go alongside the *Ole Wegger* toward 0530 hours on January 13 to collect oil and blubber.

The first facsimile tells of the *Pinguin*'s commander's decisions and how he put them into effect.

The events related in the second facsimile took place shortly before midnight on January 13. The *Pinguin*'s course of action was clear to her commander: to wait and take the *Solglimt* by surprise. 25 minutes later he was able to note his success.

The third facsimile covers events on the evening of January 14, including the seizure of the factory ship *Pelagos* and a large part of her fleet of catchers.

The final result of the night's work was the capture of the factory ships *Ole Wegger* and *Pelagos,* the depot ship *Solglimt* and 11 catchers, each of between 249 and 361 GRT. The *Ole Wegger* was found to be carrying 7,000 tons of whale oil and 5,500 tons of fuel oil. Her crew numbered around 190 and she was provisioned for ten weeks. At ten knots she consumed 45 tons of fuel each day. Three of her catchers managed to escape.

The *Solglimt* had taken on 4,000 tons of whale oil and had 4,000 tons of fuel oil left. She was carrying 60 men and had accommodation for another 300, with provisions for ten weeks. She had been fitted with a gun platform while in neutral Montevideo, but there was no gun mounted on it.

The *Pelagos* was carrying 9,500 tons of whale oil

*Three of the whale catchers captured with the* Solglimt *and* Ole Wegger.

and 800 tons of fuel oil and had a crew of 210. At 11 knots she used 60 tons of fuel a day and likewise was provisioned for ten weeks.

Also found by officers of the boarding party on the *Ole Wegger* was a 4-inch gun and two other weapons of the same calibre, one of which was intended for the *Pelagos,* together with 300 rounds of ammunition for each.

Papers discovered on board the captured ships indicated that they were the property of the Royal Norwegian Government in exile, based in England, and could therefore be sunk or sent back to Germany as prizes. The masters of the factory ships, who were jointly in charge of the whaling fleet, were ordered to process the whales already caught, with the promise of settlement.

On January 15 radio traffic between the factory ship *Thorshammer* and her catchers was intercepted. It was assumed, correctly as it transpired, that those of the *Ole Wegger*'s catchers which had escaped had raised the alarm and that pursuit would not be worth while.

The *Pinguin* now began to assemble her captures around the *Pelagos* while considering what best to do with them. The *Pelagos,* as the vessel that looked least like a factory ship, was to be the first for despatch to Western France. She was to take aboard the *Solglimt*'s whale oil and top-up her fuel oil from her. The *Solglimt* was to follow and details were settled at a conference between the prize officers and the ships' masters. Two days were devoted to preparations for the homeward trip, during which interval the *Pinguin* radioed a situation report from a distant point, making it difficult for enemy direction finding equipment to locate her.

The three large ships reached the French Atlantic coast without incident. Nine catchers arrived after a somewhat adventurous trip and were later used as submarine hunters and minesweepers. Two others were stopped near Gibraltar by British naval forces and sunk by their crews. One of these, the *Star XXIV,* had already been examined by the British and allowed to proceed as there appeared to be nothing untoward about her. However, when her sister the *Star XIV* scuttled herself in full view of the British, the crew of *Star XXIV* feared renewed interest. They were right, and accordingly followed the *Star XIV*'s example. One catcher, the *Pol IX,* was retained by the *Pinguin* as a reconnaissance

**Facsimile of extract from *Pinguin*'s log**

12.1: *According to intercepted wireless messages,* Solglimt *is apparently to go alongside* Ole Wegger *towards 0530 hours. The last radioed position indicates that I am about 70 sea miles from them.*

*Around mid-day proceeded southeast to obtain a westerly bearing.*

2200 hours: *On a westerly course.*

2315 hours: *White lights bearing two degrees to port.*

1200 hours: *56°45' S 04°33' W, NW by N 3, Sea 2–3, obscure, snow and fog, moderate visibility.*

*I stayed in a position about 70 nautical miles northeast of the* Ole Wegger. *Although the two ships were together to-day from about 1000 hours I decided to delay capture until the two 12,000-tonners were alongside each other so that they would be as good as unmanoeuverable and the prize crews could take them more easily. I had to take into account also that the tanker* Solglimt *will have been armed for her Atlantic trip. When lying alongside another vessel freedom for the use of her guns would be restricted.*

2000 hours: Ole Wegger *and* Solglimt *agree to go alongside each other early next morning about 0400 hours.*

**13.1.**

Etwas später sind viele Lichter der beiden
großen längsseitliegenden Schiffe und daneben
einzelner Fangboote auszumachen.

Kurz darauf kommt in einer Schneeboe alles
aus Sicht und bleibt für ca. 45 Min. verschwunden.

Wir können uns daher völlig ungesehen
nähern.

**14.1.**
**0015ʰ**

klart es auf. "Pinguin" steht unmittelbar bei
den Schiffen.

**0020ʰ**

Scheinwerfer leuchten, Aussetzen der Boote.

Die Schiffe, die im Scheine unzähliger
Decklampen und Tiefstrahler mit mehreren
Walen zwischen sich längsseit liegen, werden
einmal abgeleuchtet, um so die Anwesenheit
eines Kriegsschiffes zu dokumentieren. Ein
Schuß wird vorläufig nicht abgegeben, um die
wie im tiefsten Frieden arbeitenden Leute nicht
unnötig nervös zu machen und die Fangboote
nicht aufzuscheuchen.

Mehrere Male absetzen des Morsespruchs
"Do not use wireless and telefone.
We send a boat !"

Inzwischen sind 2 Prisenkommandos in 2 Booten
längsseit.

Die Maschine meldet, nachdem das Schiff
gestoppt hat, einen Motor unklar, ein Cylinder
macht Wasser. Aufnehmen des Cylinders wird sofort begonnen, es wird Riß im Cylinderdeckel
festgestellt.

**0045ʰ**

Morsespruch :
"Schiffe sind in unseren Händen !"

---

**2209ʰ**

taucht hinter Eisfeldern, die in der einsetzenden Dunkelheit erst umfahren werden müssen,
voraus ein weisses Licht auf. Es ist dies eins
der "Pelagos"-Boote, das westlich von ihm bei
Walflaggen liegt. Es wird in 3 - 4 sm Abstand
passiert, in der Annahme, daß die Besatzung
schläft. Tatsächlich erfolgt nichts.
Seit

**2255ʰ**

sind mehrere weitere Lichter voraus zu sehen,
die bald als die der in vollem Betrieb und hell
erleuchteten Kocherei ausgemacht werden. Mit
Höchstfahrt bis 200 m an das Schiff, in dessen
Nähe 5 Fangboote liegen, herangefahren, und um

**2400ʰ**

zugleich mit Booteaussetzen, den Morsespruch
abgegeben, nicht zu funken oder zu telefonieren.

**15.1.**

Die Inbesitznahme der Kocherei gelingt reibungslos. Ein Fangboot, welches zusammen mit
"Pinguin" bei der Kocherei anlangte, wird nach
Morseaufforderung zu stoppen, unmittelbar neben
uns vom Verkehrsboot besetzt und mit diesem
Fangboot die abgeteilten Kommandos auf weitere
Fangboote abgesetzt.

Der "Pelagos"-Kapitän erhält Anweisung,
seine Boote unauffällig telefonisch zurückzurufen. Die aussenstehenden Fangboote kommen
dieser Telefonieaufforderung heranzukommen,
nach und werden jeweils gleich wahrgenommen.

---

*I decided to steer northwest during the night in order to get an exact bearing on the now stationary ships with the intention of attacking to-morrow, planning so that I approach the side free of whale-catcher craft, gaining surprise under cover of darkness.*

13.1: *Somewhat later many more lights were made out coming from the two ships lying alongside each other and from several adjacent catchers.*

*Shortly afterwards everything was blotted out in a snow squall which lasted about 45 minutes.*

*We expected to be able to approach completely unobserved.*

14.1, 0015 hours: *It cleared up. The* Pinguin *hard by the two ships.*

0020 hours: *Searchlights switched on and boats swung out.*

*The ships with their numerous deck lights and sundry whales lying between them were suddenly illuminated in a way that left no doubt but that a warship was present. No warning shot was fired in order that the flensers, etc, quietly at their jobs should not be startled unnecessarily or the catcher-vessels scared away.*

*Repeatedly despatched in morse: 'Do not use wireless and telephone, we send a boat!'*

*In the meantime two prize-commandos went alongside in two boats.*

*The engine room reported, after the ship had stopped, that a motor was out of action, water entering one cylinder. A start was made at once on dismantling it and a crack was found in the casing.*

0045 hours: *Morse message: 'The ships are in our hands!'*

2209 hours: *. . . behind icefields which, in the gathering darkness, had first to be sailed around, ahead, a white light. It was a boat from the* Pelagos *lying alongside 'flagged' whale carcases. It was passed three or four miles distant—presumably the crew were asleep. Nothing actually followed.*

2255 hours: *More lights were seen ahead which were soon made out as a brightly-lit factory ship in full operation. We went at full speed up to within 200 metres of it where five 'catchers' were cruising around and at the same time (2400 hours) as putting our boats out ordered in Morse that radio and radio telephone should not be used.*

15.1: *Possession of the factory ship was achieved without resistance. A 'catcher', which had arrived alongside the factory ship with the* Pinguin, *after being ordered to stop sending in Morse, was stationed directly next to us by our duty-boat and this 'catcher' was used to round up others and put commandos aboard.*

*The master of the* Pelagos *was instructed to recall his boats in a way that would not arouse suspicion. They duly complied and were likewise one by one accounted for.*

**Above** *The whale factory ship* Ole Wegger *arrives at Bordeaux. The two athwartships funnels and goalpost masts identify her function.*

**Left** *The* Pelagos *lacked many of the usual distinguishing features of a factory ship and was for this reason the first ship of the captured whaling fleet to be sent back to France. She too arrived safely at Bordeaux.*

craft to extend her range of search. After the *Pinguin*'s sinking she was attached first to the supply ship *Alstertor* and then to the auxiliary cruiser *Komet* which commissioned her as a minelayer to operate the New Zealand waters. After this the *Komet* used her as a target ship for gunnery practice and sank her on July 1 1941.

The value to Germany of the *Pinguin*'s haul was considerable, particularly the whale oil which was used in the manufacture of margarine. These vital supplies and the fuel oil made the prospects much brighter for the *Pinguin* and other auxiliary cruisers in continuing their war against enemy seaborne trade.

**Right** *The factory ship* Ole Wegger *arrives at a French port. The open stern and slipway, through which the whale carcases were hauled aboard for cutting up, appear to have been painted out by a German censor.*

**Below** *A catcher comes alongside the* Pinguin *using a whale carcase as a fender.*

# Leisure

There could be weeks or even months of deadly boredom aboard an auxiliary cruiser. This might be because no victim could be found, or because the ship's operational area had had to be changed. Another auxiliary cruiser might have a particular project in hand which could not be disturbed, as might one's own ship, especially if her machinery needed overhaul. A commander may have stopped his ship for a time, thinking it perhaps best to lie low pending enemy reaction to his latest attack.

Even the officers, who could generally be regarded as party to their commander's train of thought, might find it difficult to forbear as the days wore on without anything worth while presenting itself for attention. It can well be imagined that in this atmosphere petty officers and men would begin to lose faith in their seniors. That would be the time for the commander to step in. Without revealing his future intentions (which might involuntarily be disclosed under interrogation by anyone who became a prisoner-of-war), he would speak plainly to his men. He should feel able to join in the occasional joke and unbend by taking part in crossing-the-line ceremonies and sporting events, lectures and perhaps the sponsoring of a ship's newspaper.

Crewmen aboard auxiliary cruisers were allowed, according to circumstances, to practice their own pet hobbies, such as music, painting, wood-carving, sports of different kinds and reading, not to a laid-down programme but as their fancy took them. Each ship carried a well-stocked library as well as films and projectors. The radio room was equipped to play music over the public address system as well as to broadcast orders. The wireless request programmes, so popular in wartime Germany, could be heard in mid-ocean.

The German Army is traditionally able to allow marriage by proxy, and this privilege was extended to include the personnel of auxiliary cruisers, even though a ship might be anywhere between Africa and Australia. Mail delivery was rare enough, let alone opportunities for the parties to meet together, so there was legal provision for marriage, the ship's commander taking the role of registrar.

To forge and maintain a high morale on board at all times necessitated a dialogue between man and man without regard to rank or appointment, creating mutual trust together with the upholding of perfect discipline. The fostering of this dialogue, next to care of the ship and adherence to its standards, was the first duty of senior officers.

There was even 'leave' aboard auxiliary cruisers during the Second World War, that is to say a complete freedom from all duties for a set period, except during an 'alarm'.

**Left** *After her long voyage, a whale catcher ties up in a French harbour alongside her sister vessel.*

**Right** *A sailor on watch cannot allow his attention to be diverted. In his leisure time he can enjoy undisturbed such sights as frolicking dolphins* (Stier).

**Above** *Crossing-the-line cere-
mony aboard the* Kronprinz Wilhelm. *Neptune is flanked by his
queen, Thetis, and his secretary
(wearing a stock exchange
bowler). The senior members of
the ship's company form an
appreciative audience.*

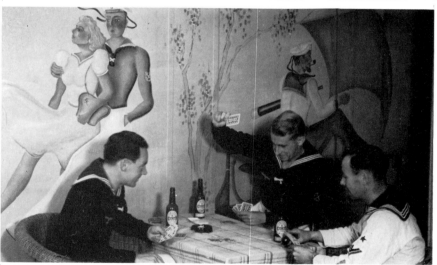

**Left** *A lively hand of cards in the*
Orion*'s reading and games room.*

**Left** *During his leisure time on
board, this man built a model of
the training barque* Horst Wessel
(Orion).

# Supply

The availability of fuel played a decisive part in auxiliary cruiser operations, except in the unusual case of the *Seeadler* which was a sailing vessel. The converted express steamers of 1914 were particularly affected as each vesssel's coal consumption ran to something like 350 tons a day. Each would have a capacity of around 3,000 tons which was equal only to the needs of her usual peacetime route. As cruisers these vessels were required to range much further afield and, in an effort to ensure that they had sufficient bunkers, their interiors were ruthlessly gutted to provide space for coal chutes and other means of transporting the fuel. The coal ports in their hull sides were useless for refuelling at sea and had to be replaced by openings in their decks. Handling gear which had hitherto catered for items little more substantial than passengers' luggage and light cargo, had to be hastily adapted to move coal. Even then, wind conditions only a little above Force Three could cause mutual damage to ships lying alongside each other. The *Kronprinz Wilhelm* had to cope with all these problems for many months before being beaten in the end through a lack of fresh food.

Other ships faced the same problems but, when supplies ran out, there was nothing for it but to run for a neutral port, there to be interned, as were the *Cormoran* and *Prinz Eitel Friedrich*. The later coal-burning auxiliary cruisers had things somewhat easier as additional bunker capacity was created by converting the holds, provided they were not required for other urgent purposes. The cargo handling gear was adapted to take supplies aboard in nets, sacks or slings, and crews got used to these arrangements. Even so a heavy swell could interfere with operations.

**Below left** *October 28 1914. The* Kronprinz Wilhelm *tows the French four-masted barque* Union *into calmer waters. In the meantime a working party is preparing for the transfer of her cargo of coal, stepping down the iron yards and topmasts and clearing the decks of anything that might obstruct the operation. On November 2 the* Kronprinz Wilhelm *attempted to bring the* Union *alongside under Force Six conditions, the urgency dictated by the former vessel's coal stocks having fallen to a mere 350 tons. Three days later the weather eased up. On November 6, after much effort, 45 tons were transferred, later increasing to 300 tons. It had been a back-breaking job.* **Below** *Aboard the* Union *a hand-operated capstan is used to get the coal out of the hold. Some idea of the task can be gained from the fact that the auxiliary cruiser's crew, of whom 95 per cent were reservists, worked at it for 70 of the 248 days that their ship was in commission.*

**Left** *It was a comparatively easy matter to transfer coal from a steamer with her power-operated winches. In this photo the* Möwe *is being coaled from the* Saint Theodore *before the latter was herself fitted out and commissioned as the auxiliary cruiser* Geier. *The* Möwe *took what remained of the* Geier's *coal before she had to sink her on February 14 1917.*

**Below** *Following a transfer of oil fuel aboard the* Widder, *the pipeline is run aft to be uncoupled and stowed away. The manila cable lies partly under the pipe.*

During the early days of the First World War things worked reasonably well but they began to get difficult after a month or two. It was then the enemy who helped, coal being taken from seized vessels, a source of supply which the auxiliary cruisers had to manage with from the autumn of 1914, or become immobilised. Often the captured coal was found to be of such poor quality that it had not been worth the trouble of taking it aboard.

The problems that had to be faced each day are described in the graphic report of the *Kronprinz Wilhelm*'s daily coal consumption and replenishment, which appears in *Der Krieg zur See 1914–1918—Der Kreuzerkrieg in den auslandischen Gewassern (The War at Sea 1914–1918—cruiser operations in distant waters)*, by Kapitänleutnant Thierfelder, who was the youngest of the German auxiliary cruiser captains in that war. His decisions were largely dictated by the fuel situation.

Between the wars the scene changed with the transition from coal to oil and the adoption of the diesel engine. So it came about that, of all the ships intercepted during the Second World War, only one was a coal burner and one, incidentally, a large sailing vessel. With oil as the motive force the responsibility of the engine room staffs increased, for oil-fired boilers and diesel engines are more prone to suffer from defects than coal-fired installations.

Modern machinery was also sensitive to the chemical composition of fuel and, with this in mind, a sample of each type of oil taken from a tanker or from the bunkers of an intercepted vessel, was first analysed on board the auxiliary cruiser to ensure its suitability for use. If the result of the analysis was satisfactory, arrangements would be made to transfer the precious liquid to the auxiliary cruiser or one of her escorts.

Lubricating oil was usually in casks, but what could amount to anything between 100 and 1,000 tons of boiler or diesel oil would have to be pumped across through a pipeline. As a rule the auxiliary cruiser would moor alongside the captured tanker or dry cargo vessel, and when danger threatened the cruiser's commander would have to decide whether to cast off or sever the lines. A 'messenger' line would usually be thrown or fired across first and then used to haul over a thick manila towline. If a ship was not prepared for this manoeuvre, her crew would be required to haul aboard a line to which the oil pipeline was attached, this being made fast to a floating line. The closed end of the pipe was then hauled over the stern and connected to the nearest valve leading into the fuel oil system. The oil was then pumped into the auxiliary cruiser. As soon as the required quantity had been delivered, the pipe would be disconnected and its end closed. It was

**Below** *The* Orion *tows the tanker* Winnetou *at a slow pace in order to ease her situation in the heavy seas.*
**Below right** *Rolling gently in the wake of* Orion, *the prize vessel* Tropic Sea *signals that the pipeline has fractured and the crew of a boat from the raider is preparing to deal with the damage. The floating cable which carries the pipeline can be seen as a thickening of the curve to the left of the latter.*

then hauled back aboard the raider and 'run in', the men detailed for the job taking the pipe over the bow and running aft with it, uncoupling it from the standpipe and taking in the floating line. If the raider was being refuelled from one of the German Navy's own tankers the link from the latter would be over the stern of the raider because there would be more room on the tanker for the pipe to be laid out.

Whatever the means of transfer, each ship had to be able to move so as to compensate for untoward drifting by the other, or both towline and oil pipe-line could fracture. Manoeuvring could be time-consuming and thus increase the period at risk, especially as the raider would not be at readiness for instant action. An extra tight watch had to be maintained, not only during refuelling but at every rendezvous with other ships. All lookout posts had to be manned to watch closely for any evidence which might later draw attention to the ship's presence there, such as a leak in the pipeline or a box dropped into the sea.

In bad weather both raider and supply ship had

to position themselves accordingly. In storm or hurricane conditions one or the other might have to heave-to, maintaining just sufficient power to keep her head into the sea and steerage way on, while the transfer was being effected. An example of this was the refuelling of the pocket battleship *Deutschland* by the naval oiler *Nordmark* in September 1939 in the Davis Strait, between Greenland and Canada. On this occasion the wind strength was 12 with a Force Nine Sea.

If supplies other than oil had to be transferred, such as food, shells, torpedoes or aircraft, and it was considered prudent, auxiliary cruiser and supply ship could lie alongside each other, thus avoiding the wearisome business of boating material between the two. This also shortened the period of maximum risk. Such encounters provided an opportunity for the exchange of views, ideas and experiences between the respective commanders.

The supply ship would bring eagerly awaited letters from home and the opportunity to mail letters back. The latter had to be most carefully composed lest they should fall into enemy hands

**Left** *The naval oiler* Uckermark *served the pocket battleship* Admiral Graf Spee *under her original name of* Altmark. *She is best known for having been intercepted by the British destroyer* Cossack, *during which encounter a large number of British prisoners-of-war were released. The* Uckermark *was later employed furnishing auxiliary cruisers with supplies from Germany and Japan. She blew up at Yokohama on November 30 1941 as a result, it is believed, of inadequate tank cleaning. The* Thor *and the supply ship* Leuthen *were also destroyed in the fire which followed the blast.*

**Left** *Rendezvous in the South Atlantic on June 21 1942. The tanker* Charlotte Schliemann *can be seen to the left, with the supply ship and blockade runner* Doggerbank *(the former* Speybank, *captured by* Atlantis *on January 31 1941 and ordered back to Germany) on the right. Part of the* Michel *can be seen in the foreground.*

and give anything away.

The *Seekriegsleitung*'s network of supply ships was worldwide. As the war progressed it became apparent that no similar organisation of such efficiency had ever existed before, with all its meeting points for the supply ships, auxiliary cruisers and their prizes.

Disclosure of a rendezvous' location could be fatal. Should a thoroughly bad one have been chosen as, for instance, at the intersection of main trade routes, the risk of discovery was increased immeasurably. This happened when the *Seekriegsleitung* ordered the auxiliary cruiser *Atlantis* to refuel the *U-126*. The two were discovered by the British 'County' Class cruiser HMS *Devonshire* with the result that the *Atlantis* received such damage that she had to be abandoned.

Sometimes it was necessary for an auxiliary cruiser to transfer supplies to other ships from her own stocks. Occasionally an auxiliary cruiser would take out supplies for transfer to U-boats, as when the *Pinguin* carried torpedoes for delivery to the U-boat *UA*.

**Above** *It is all hands to help when supplies arrive and have to be stowed.*

**Below** *An auxiliary cruiser serving as a supply ship. The U-boat* UA *approaches the* Pinguin *to take aboard torpedoes which the latter has brought for her. July 18 1940*

# Maintenance

The landsman takes the word 'ship' to mean that which lies between keel and truck and between jackstaff and taffrail, but to the sailor at sea it encompasses his whole world. Neglected, one day it could ensnare him.

The upkeep of an auxiliary cruiser was the entire responsibility of the first officer, as was the execution of necessary repairs. Each ship was equipped with workshops staffed by technicians and specialists in well-nigh every trade, their inventiveness repeatedly postponing the day when their commander might have to decide to make for home because of a mechanical breakdown or other trouble which was more than could be put right from resources on board. Since a machinery overhaul temporarily condemned the ship to inactivity, some remote island with good anchor-

*Work on the hull while at sea: the* Michel *is receiving a new and darker shade of paint.*

holding ground would be sought where it could be carried out. This would also provide an opportunity for the crew to stretch their legs, drink fresh water and enjoy the sight of something green other than the screen of the starboard light. The engines would be stripped down, replacement parts fitted and the results of tests anxiously awaited. The deck crew, if they were not required to help out in the engine room, would use the time to attend to hull, super-structure, rigging and boats. The hull plating would receive special attention because little could be done to it while the ship was at sea, repainting to vary a disguise normally having to take place at night. In an island hide-out the old paint could be chipped off and the metal treated to inhibit rust. Living and leisure spaces, galleys and toilets, all received the same attention as officers' messes, canteens, magazines and bread stores.

Next in importance would be the thorough daily or weekly attention to armament, changing of bed linen, inspection of the men's eating utensils (mess tins) for absolute cleanliness, and much more.

Supply ships from Germany or Japan would bring material to these secluded spots which it would be very difficult or even impossible to transfer at sea, such as replacement aircraft or unwieldy machine spares.

Obviously security would have to be in accordance with the surroundings. Lookouts and alarm posts would be manned against surpise attack. The ship's aircraft would patrol, contacting approaching supply vessels and directing them to the area with instructions dropped in pouches. On arrival their crews would see the unusual spectacle of what almost amounted to a ship repair yard.

Eventually anchor would have to be weighed and the cruiser war resumed, leaving behind as little evidence as possible of the visit. For all that, the grave of a comrade accidentally killed would be clearly marked.

Memories of carefree days under palm trees, on reefs or in the warm waters of lagoons would soon fade. So too would those of hours spent on lookout from the highest point of an island, all to be replaced by thoughts of the next landfall: home!

**Above** *The supply ship* Anneliese Essberger, *disguised as a Japanese Kawasaki vessel. She was a motorship of 5,173 GRT built in 1935 and sunk in 1942.*

**Right** *The* Kronprinz Wilhelm *in drydock whilst interned. Normally divers undertook such underwater work as repairs to hull damage, adjustment of propeller blades and the plugging of those leaks which could not be reached from inside.*

**Below** *Finishing Iron Crosses whose awards have been advised by radio. Knight's Crosses were similarly produced for commanders.*

**Below right** *An unforgettable memory: sand, sun and bananas in abundance.*

# Action

The word 'cruiser' covers the heavy, light, armoured and battle cruiser as well as the unprotected cruiser and, last but not least, the auxiliary cruiser. In both world wars German auxiliary cruisers made contact with all of them. The British armed merchant cruiser was almost on a par with the conventional warship. She was faster and more heavily armed than her German opposite number and, during the First World War, British auxiliaries accounted for three German commerce raiders: the *Carmania* against the *Cap Trafalgar* on September 14 1914; the *Alcantara* and *Andes* against the *Greif* on February 29 1916, in which action the *Alcantara* was sunk by the *Greif;* and the armed boarding vessel *Dundee* which, with the regular cruiser HMS *Achilles*, sank the *Leopard* on March 16 1917. On the other hand the German auxiliary cruiser *Meteor* sank the armed boarding vessel *The Ramsey* on August 8 1915 by torpedo attack at a range of 600 metres, but managed to rescue 46 of her complement of 98.

There were other incidents involving British and German auxiliary warships. In September 1915 the British AMC *Himalaya* captured two colliers on their way to fuel the German auxiliary cruiser *Cormoran,* and in consequence the *Cormoran* had to seek internment when she ran short of fuel. On December 25 1916 the British AMC *Avenger* stopped and searched the auxiliary cruiser *Seeadler*, did not find anything suspicious and sailed away after wishing the raider a pleasant voyage! On February 16 1917 the AMC *Edinburgh Castle* shadowed the auxiliary cruiser *Möwe* until she vanished into a rain squall and escaped.

More than once during the Second World War German and British auxiliaries came in sight of each other but did not exchange fire. On June 24 1941 the *Pinguin* was disturbed while minelaying off Madras by the appearance of the AMC *Canton*. A reported sighting of the *Shenking* nine days earlier remains unconfirmed. The *Shenking*, a former China Navigation Company vessel, was actually serving the Royal Air Force as depot ship for flying boats in the Indian Ocean.

Only the *Thor* actually came to battle with AMCs, and this on three occasions. On July 28 1940 she engaged the *Alcantara* (22,209 GRT), inflicting damage and herself suffering three killed and three wounded. On December 5 1940 she took on the *Carnarvon Castle* (20,122 GRT) in a sharp engagement, scoring 20 hits without harm to herself. The *Carnarvon Castle* on the other hand

*The passenger liner* Voltaire *(Lamport & Holt Line, Liverpool; 13,245 GRT, 15 kts, 624 passengers) was the third armed merchant cruiser to be engaged by the* Thor, *this time in a fight to the finish. It was touch and go for the German auxiliary cruiser but she sank the* Voltaire *without casualties to herself and rescued three-quarters of her opponent's complement.*

| Datum und Uhrzeit | Angabe des Ortes, Wind, Wetter, Seegang, Beleuchtung, Sichtigkeit der Luft, Mondschein usw. | Vorkommnisse |
|---|---|---|
| 0450 Uhr | Sonnenaufgang,diesig | |
| 0531 Uhr | | In 45° etwa 4 sm ab erscheint plötzlich aus dem Dunst ein sehr grosser Dampfer, der sofort als ein britischer Hilfskreuzer angesprochen wird, vermutlich, Carnavon Castle. |
| | | Ich drehe nach BB. ab, in der Hoffnung, in dem diesigen Wetter unterzuschneiden. Es hat auch zuerst den Anschein. Der Dampfer hält seinen Kurs durch und sackt achteraus. Leider wird die Sicht etwas besser und auf etwa 140 hm dreht der Dampfer hinter mir auf nach *Südwest* ~~Norden~~. Die Sicht schwankt zwischen 140 und 170 hm. Der Dampfer folgt. Die Entfernung steht bei etwa 160 hm. |
| | | Ich lasse es dahingestellt, ob der Dampfer, wenn ich meinen Kurs durchgehalten hätte- ich führte die jugoslawischen Hoheits= zeichen an der Bordwand- auch seinerseits weitergefahren wäre. Ich glaube es nicht. Offenbar wurde der Kommandant erst verständigt und hat dann sofort aufgedreht. |
| | | Meine Hoffnung auf Nebel erfüllte sich nicht. Es muss zum Kampf kommen. |
| 0533 Uhr | Wind NNw 3.See 2. bedeckt diesig. | Alarm. Maschine Äusserste Kraft |
| | | Die Entfernung stand eine ganze Weile, offenbar hatte der Geg= ner noch nicht alle *Notoren* in Betrieb. Bald jedoch lief er langsam auf und machte mit Scheinwerfer "SC" ~~gleich:~~ zeigen Sie Ihr Unter= scheidungssignal und bald darauf "K" ~~gleich:~~ Stoppen Sie sofort. |
| *0701* ~~0659~~ Uhr | | Um 0*701* ~~659~~ Uhr schoß er einen Schuß, der etwa 300 m kurz lag. Er stand zu dieser Zeit in meinem Kielwasser. |
| 0702 Uhr | | Ich beschloß zunächst ein Heckgefecht zu führen und eröffnete zu= nächst um 0702 Uhr mit Setzen der Kriegsflagge das Feuer. E= 129 hm. |

**Facsimile of extract from *Thor*'s log of November 11 1940**
0450 hours: *Sunrise, hazy.*

0531 hours: *Bearing 45° distance four nautical miles there suddenly appeared a very large steamer which was immediately taken to be a British auxiliary cruiser, presumably the* Carnarvon Castle.

*I turned to port in the hope of cutting him off in the hazy weather. At first he seemed to do the same. The steamer held on to her course and disappeared. Unfortunately the visibility improved and at about 140 hm the steamer turned astern of me to the southwest. The visibility fluctuated between 140 and 170 hm. The steamer followed . . . The distance remained constant at about 160 hm.*

*I could not tell whether the steamer, should I hold my course, would do the same—I was displaying Yugoslav colours on my hull—I did not think so. He seemed to be doing the obvious thing and then changing his mind.*

*My hopes of fog were not fulfilled. It was going to come to a fight.*

0533 hours: *Wind NW 3, Sea 2, Overlying haze: Alarm. Maximum power from engines.*

*The distance remained constant for quite a while; apparently the enemy's engines were not in full operation. Soon however he gradually increased his speed and made the signal 'SC' with his searchlight: 'give your identification signal' and soon after: 'K': 'stop at once'.*

0701 hours: *About 0701 hours he fired a shot which landed about 300 m short. At this time he lay in my wake.*

0702 hours: *I decided first of all to fight from astern and opened fire at 0702 hours at the same time hoisting my naval ensign. Distance = 129 hm.*

(continued overleaf)

```
        Nach den ersten Salven, deren Beobachtung durch das diesige
Wetter stark behindert wurde, drehte der Gegner nach BB. ab, um sei=
ne Breitseite ins Gefecht zu bringen. Ich drehte allmählich nach
St.B. auf zum ~~Drehlos~~gefecht, um womöglich die Lee-Stellung und zu=
gleich die Sonne im Rücken zu gewinnen. Der Gegner schoss in unre=
gelmässigen Zeitabschnitten Einzelschüsse aus offenbar 4/15 cm
Geschützen und aus 2 Geschützen kleineren Kalibers. Um sein Ein=
schiessen zu Erschweren, seine ersten Schüsse lagen weit und der
Seite nach gut, ließ ich für kurze Zeit die Bugnebelanlage anstellen,
Leider arbeitete das Abstellen nicht sofort, so daß etwa 5 Minuten
lang die achteren Geschütze das Ziel nicht erfassen konnten.
        Trotz der schwierigen Beobachtungsverhältnisse durch Nebel,
Mündungsqualm und künstlichem Nebel lag die eigene Batterie sehr
bald gut am Ziel. Der A.O. schoss nach der E.ß.-Uhr.
        Der Gegner lief mit hoher Fahrt ( 21 sm erkoppelt) nach Westen.
langsam nördlich drehend. So konnte ich im Kreisgefecht die günsti=
ge Wind= und Sonnenseite gewinnen.
0753 Uhr        Da ich annahme, dass der Gegner nach Osten laufen würde, dreh=
        te ich auch auf 90° und brachte die BB.Seite ins Gefecht.( E 95 -
        87 hm).
        Inzwischen waren bei einigen Geschützen die Rohre so heiss ge=
worden, dass sie in den Wiegen klemmten und nicht ganz in Feuer=
stellung liefen. Bei 2 Geschützen leckten die Bremszylinder, das
Richten wurde dadurch sehr erschwert. Die Streuung in den Salven
nahm erheblich zu. Der Munitionsverbrauch, der ohnehin hoch war,
wurde dadurch gesteigert. Trotzdem blieb die Batterie am Ziel.
~~Weitere~~ Treffer wurden ~~nicht sicher~~ beobachtet, sind aber wahrschein=
lich.
0802 Uhr        dreht der Gegner, der immer noch mit unverminderter Geschwindig=
        keit läuft, dessen Einschläge jedoch wohl in Folge schlechter Be=
        obachtungsverhältnisse alle sehr weit liegen, plötzlich hart nach
        Norden ab. Er wirft einige Nebelbojen, feuert aus 2 Heckgeschützen
        noch einige Schüsse und ist um 0815 Uhr im Dunst aus Sicht.
```

*After the first rounds, observation of the result of which was hindered by the hazy weather, the enemy turned to port to bring her broadside to bear. I turned slowly to starboard to benefit if possible from a lee position and at the same time to have the sun behind me. The enemy fired single shots at irregular intervals apparently from four 15 cm [6-inch] guns and two smaller pieces. To confuse his range, his first shots went wide. I had the forward smoke screen operated for a short time. Unfortunately this did not cut off immediately so that for about five minutes the after guns could not be brought to bear on the target.*

*Notwithstanding the difficulty of observation through fog, gun smoke and our own artificial smoke, the one battery very soon fastened on to the target. The gunnery officer was firing according to the rate of range clock.*

*The enemy made off at high speed (21 knots) to the westward, slowly veering north, so I was able to take advantage in the running fight of the wind and direction of the sun.*

0753 hours: *As I had assumed that the enemy would turn eastwards I turned 90° and brought my port side to bear in the engagement (distance 95–87 hm).*

*In the meantime the barrels of some of the guns had become so hot that they had jammed in their mountings and could not be brought to bear. The brake cylinders of two of them leaked and considerably hindered their direction. Dispersal of the salvos increased considerably. Expenditure of ammunition, already very high, was increased in this way. Nevertheless the battery held on to its target. Three hits were observed; there were probably more.*

0802 hours: *The enemy turned suddenly hard to the north with undiminished speed. His shots had been wide because of the poor visibility. He threw a few smoke floats, fired a few rounds from two stern guns and at about 0815 hours was out of sight in the haze.*

lost 37 killed and had 82 wounded. On April 4 1941 the *Thor* sank the *Voltaire* after an hour-long fight, rescuing three-quarters of the latter's complement.

The thoughts and reactions of the *Thor*'s commander could not be better expressed than in the extracts from his log of December 5 1940 which are reproduced on pages 113 and 114. He cautiously notes only three confirmed hits whereas *Thor* actually achieved 20.

Actions during the First World War involving British regular cruisers and German auxiliary cruisers understandably resulted in successes for the regular cruisers: on August 26 1914 the protected cruiser HMS *Highflyer* (5,700 tons, 11 6-inch [15.2-cm] guns) attacked the German auxiliary cruiser *Kaiser Wilhelm der Große* as she lay in neutral waters. The appearance of British naval forces on March 5 1917 caused the commander of the auxiliary cruiser *Iltis* to scuttle his ship; he had completed his minelaying tasks and armed resistance would have been hopeless. The previous night he had succeeded in outwitting the light cruiser HMS *Fox*. Other types of British cruiser had only an indirect influence on the activities of the German auxiliary cruisers during the First World War.

In the unequal Second World War battles between regular and auxiliary cruisers, the raiders had little chance of survival. The sinking of the *Pinguin* by the 'County' Class cruiser HMS *Cornwall* on May 8 1941 raised the curtain on this kind of action. A broadside of eight 8-inch (20.3 cm) guns was trained on only four 15-cm guns. The *Pinguin* was posing as a Norwegian at the time when the *Cornwall* came within her range. Hits were scored but the tide of battle soon turned. Kapitän zur See Krüder had already decided to abandon and scuttle his ship when a partial salvo (four rounds) from the British vessel enveloped her, striking, among other points, the arsenal of 130 mines waiting to be laid. They exploded, blowing the *Pinguin* to pieces. The *Cornwall* was able to pick up 60 men of whom only 23 survived.

The next action between a regular and an auxiliary cruiser took place six months and 11 days later, on November 19 1941, and involved the Australian vessel HMAS *Sydney* and the *Kormoran*. With eight 6-inch (15.2 cm) guns, the *Sydney* was classed as a 'light' cruiser. The cat and mouse game between the suspicious Australian and auxiliary cruiser commander Detmers lasted several hours, the latter only too aware of his ship's inferiority should it come to a fight. Then his opportunity arrived: the cruiser came within range of the *Kormoran*'s two above-water torpedo tubes. If anything was to be done it had to be done then, and quickly. Her guns were trained on the *Sydney*'s vulnerable points. The torpedoes were released as the battle ensign was hoisted, shells thundered across and machine-gun fire raked the cruiser's decks. The *Sydney* tried to take avoiding action but it was too late. She sank in the darkness of the night, taking all on board with her. The *Kormoran* had received only two hits but one was in the engine room, severing the cable between the generator and the main engines, so she had to be abandoned. 76 men had been killed and their bodies went down with the ship. Survivors reached the Australian coast in boats or on rafts, suffering from hunger, thirst and wounds.

Only three days later, on November 22, the *Atlantis* was ordered to refuel a U-boat at a rendezvous which her commander, Kapitän zur See Rogge, did not consider secure. The refuelling operation proceeded quickly in the hope that the spot could be safely and speedily vacated, but the 'County' Class cruiser HMS *Devonshire* appeared and opened fire from outside the range of the *Atlantis*' guns. Escape was out of the question as the cruiser could achieve at least 30 knots against *Atlantis*' maximum of 16. In a little less than an hour the cruiser would overhaul the raider, provided that she was still afloat, so Rogge decided to sink his ship. The story of the eventful trip home is related elsewhere in this book. Only eight men were lost in the course of the action and subsequent sinking, a tribute to Rogge's judgement.

A final word on the two cruisers which overpowered the *Pinguin* and the *Atlantis*. They have been called 'heavy' because this type was permitted to mount guns of larger calibre than 6-inch (15.2 cm) but not greater than 8-inch (20.3 cm), in accordance with the conditions laid down by the Washington Treaty in 1922. The British insisted on building right up to the permitted displacement tonnage of 10,000. These ships could then be so fast and powerful as to be more than a match for any auxiliary cruiser, a line of thought born of lessons learned during the First World War which paid off during the Second. Their high freeboard enabled them to cruise in all weathers with little or no reduction in speed. They led the

**Left** *After her engagement with the* Thor, *the armed merchant cruiser* Carnarvon Castle *(a passenger motorship of the Union Castle Line, London; 20,122 GRT, 18 kts, 660 passengers) put into Montevideo where the bodies of the 37 men killed in the action were laid to rest.*

**Below** *The 'County' Class cruiser* Cornwall *destroyed the auxiliary cruiser* Pinguin. *The photograph shows her in peacetime, sidelights not welded over and awning stanchions in place. The eight 8-in (20.3 cm) guns had a range of over 18 miles. The high freeboard and knuckle to the forepart gave the class extraordinary seaworthiness.*

hunt for the *Bismarck,* swept the seas, destroyed German raiders and more than proved their worth in helping to keep open the British lifeline.

In both world wars there were bitter encounters between auxiliary cruisers and merchantmen. Men whom many would say were innocent passengers were killed on both sides. With one exception these engagements resulted in victory for the auxiliary cruisers. This was the action between the *Stier* under Kapitän zur See Gerlach and the American vessel *Stephen Hopkins,* one of the EC2-A-C1 type developed by and built for the US Maritime Commission. Research into American armed forces records indicates that she carried the following armament: one 6-inch (15.2 cm) gun astern, a $1\frac{1}{2}$-inch (37 mm) twin mounting forward and four machine-guns on the bridge structure, two to starboard and two to port. This disposition conflicts with the log of the *Stier* in which her commander records a very different impression of

*The Australian light cruiser* Sydney *was deceived by and fell victim to the tactics of Kapitän zur See Detmers and his crew aboard the* Kormoran. *Despite her armour, eight 6-in (15.2 cm) guns in twin turrets, powerful anti-aircraft armament, quadruple torpedo tubes port and starboard and a speed of 32 kts, she was destroyed by a converted merchantman.*

his opponent's armament:

'*At 0900 hours the enemy began to return our fire and indeed, from both our own observation and those of the* Tannenfels, *from which our adversary was also visible, firing four and sometimes five guns with good discipline. It immediately became clear that this was not an ordinary merchant ship, particularly in view of her presence in these little-frequented waters, but an auxiliary warship, patrol vessel, perhaps even an auxiliary cruiser or a troop transport, well-disguised for all that and inoffensive-looking*'.

So much for the log. What actually did happen in

**Above** *Like the* Cornwall, *the very similar* Devonshire *was a unit of the 'County' Class. With her sister ship's experience against the* Pinguin *well in mind when she engaged the* Atlantis, Devonshire *kept well out of range of the latter's 15 cm guns, which had a range of a mere 11 miles compared with the British vessel's 18.*

**Right** *The auxiliary cruiser* Stier *in the South Atlantic, a photograph taken just two days before her sinking.*

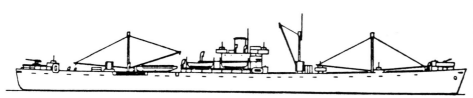

**Left** *Recognition drawing to 1:1,000 scale of the 'Liberty' Ship* Stephen Hopkins. *Type EC2-S-C1; 14,250 DT, load capacity 10,800 tons, length × breadth × depth 134.6 × 17.3 × 8.4 m, 2,500 HP, 11 kts, approximately 7,200 GRT.*

the South Atlantic on September 27 1942? The 'Liberty'-type ship was making her second voyage, from Cape Town in ballast to Paramaribo in Dutch Guinea. A change in the weather was making observation difficult. As the fog bank broke the American saw two ships lying in close proximity to each other, which her master thought looked suspicious and accordingly ordered alarm stations.

Most of the *Stier*'s crew had been occupied in trying to clean as much marine growth as possible from their ship's waterline. When signs of a deterioration in the weather were noticed, the men were recalled on deck. Only the 12-metre inflatable raft was left outboard. Visibility by this time was between one and a half and two nautical miles (3,000 to 4,000 metres). Around 0852 hours an unidentified ship was sighted some 4,000 metres distant and the engine room was ordered to make full power available. At 0853 hours the alarm was sounded throughout the ship and two minutes later the anti-aircraft and secondary armament were ordered to open fire.

*Stier* was then swept by a hail of fire, causing her commander later to enter the following in his log:

*'On the stern a 15 cm gun, forward two guns of between 10.2 cm and 12.7 cm, amidships two of this calibre forward of the funnel and two abaft it as well as a few 2 cm and 4 cm anti-aircraft guns. The enemy's fire control and discipline were shown to be very good'.*

At about 0905 hours the *Stier* received two hits, one in her steering gear and the other in her engine room. She had thus been rendered helpless a mere five minutes after the opening of the action! With no electric power all services failed. At 0910 hours she ceased fire because her opponent appeared to have been silenced, but resumed between 0913 and 0918 hours to make sure of sinking her. At 0955 hours the *Stephen Hopkins* was seen to be sinking and towards 1000 hours she disappeared. As far as could be ascertained the *Stier* had sustained 15 hits from a fairly heavy armament. She was on fire forward with flames and smoke drifting aft. By 1014 hours the main engines were running again but

the helm could only be moved between 'hard a'starboard' and 'port three degrees'. After consulting his officers Gerlach decided to abandon the *Stier* and, following the complete failure of the main engines at 1025 hours, he assembled the crew on the boat deck and told them of his decision. At about 1058 hours he gave the order to leave and the *Tannenfels* was asked to stand by. At 1140 hours the scuttling charges were ordered to be set off but, because of the fire, the midships charges could not be reached. Fuzes were set for the forward and aft charges which exploded between seven and nine minutes later. The *Stier* sank slowly, taking two of her dead with her.

The wounded were taken with the rest of the crew aboard the *Tannenfels,* where two died and were buried at sea. The *Tannenfels* then sailed for La Verdon where the *Stier*'s crew were met by Admiral Marshall, *Oberbefehlshaber* of *Marinegruppen- kommando West.*

Forty-two of the *Stephen Hopkins'* crew had been lost, 19 getting away in the one remaining serviceable boat. Five were wounded; three, it was to turn out, fatally. The survivors reached Brazil 31 days later. On the Allied side the men of the *Stephen Hopkins* were honoured—and deservedly

so for, like the men of the *Kormoran* who faced up to the *Sydney,* they had gallantly accepted a challenge knowing full well what the end would be.

But what about the *Stier?* The often pathetic-sounding log had had to be written up aboard the *Tannenfels.* Kapitän zur See Gerlach had been forced to rely upon observations made from that vessel which were not altogether reliable.

Gerlach had undoubtedly imagined his opponent to be something much more dangerous than she actually was. He spoke of good fire discipline but at the same time had not realised that the enemy ship was high out of the water and her screw therefore not fully effective. This was the reason for her low speed, not the guile of a powerful adversary trying to pass herself off as a peaceful merchantman. One might wonder why that passage in the log referring to discussions with his officers has been underscored for its full length. The casual observer could gain the impression of an attempt to shift the responsibility for decision-making on to the shoulders of others. As if the *Seekriegsleitung* would have overlooked this! Their opinion on the *Stier* incident, however, was that commander and crew had acquitted themselves 'courageously and in the best traditions of German seamanship and fighting spirit'.

**Left** *The badly damaged* Stier *was on fire in several places, the worst outbreak being forward.*

**Below** *The* Stier*'s crew watch their ship sink from the* Tannenfels. *Bad visibility had confused both sides during this engagement.*

**Right** *One of the two crewmen from the* Stier *who died aboard the* Tannenfels *is buried at sea.*

**Below** *Admiral Marschall,* Oberbefehlshaber *of* Marinegruppenkommando West, *addresses the* Stier *'s survivors aboard the* Tannenfels *on their arrival at La Verdon.*

# 'Strangers aboard!'

When this call was heard aboard a German warship in a foreign port everyone knew that danger was at hand, at least so far as the ship's secret equipment was concerned. This was all the more true in wartime when an auxiliary cruiser had on board merchant crews as civilian internees and members of enemy armed forces as prisoners of war. Certainly the presence of these people had its advantages: they could be interrogated or might involuntarily reveal information of importance, sometimes leading to the interception of other merchant vessels, or helping the auxiliary cruiser herself to escape from danger.

All in all, though, there were more drawbacks than benefits from their enforced presence. There was always the risk that a prize-vessel might be re-taken as it was sailing back to Germany, although stern measures were taken to disabuse anyone with ideas on these lines. During the First World War prisoners were put on board captured ships considered suitable for their detention. During the Second World War, with manpower at a premium, prisoners were allowed to remain wherever possible under their own administration, their officers being responsible for transmitting routine orders from the auxiliary cruiser's commander. Insofar as conditions permitted, they were afforded prepared accommodation, good feeding, medical care, regular exercise on deck and general maintenance.

In neither war were the dangers arising from 'strangers on board' under-estimated, particularly when experienced seamen came to be put ashore where they could report what they had seen. Sketches could be circulated which would help to identify their floating prisons and put the enemy on guard against the dreaded raiders. A ship's officer could use his knowledge and technical training to link his own vessel's position with that of the auxiliary cruiser and, as opportunity arose, make detailed and informative reports. Anticipating the wiles of his 'guests', an auxiliary cruiser's commander would try to give a false impression of what was happening. Rogge of the *Atlantis,* for instance, arranged 'audio camouflage' suggesting that a U-boat was being tied up alongside when in fact his ship was laying mines off the coast of South Africa.

Notwithstanding the circumstances, many personal contacts developed between captors and captives which were warmly renewed after the war. Understandably there could also be very different sentiments, hate having become too deeply rooted for reconciliation. Sadly there were casualties to mourn among the prisoners and internees. Many had lost their lives when the auxiliary cruisers aboard which they were detained were themselves hit or sunk following interception by Allied warships.

**Right** *Prisoners and internees aboard the* Pinguin *are exercised in the fresh air and daylight.*

**Below** *When the auxiliary cruiser* Wolf *arrived back in Kiel on February 24 1918, she had 467 'detainees' aboard (including eight women and two children), of whom 30 were immediately transferred to hospital. The photograph shows some of these people disembarking via one of the Kiel harbour steamers of the old Neuen Dampfer-Compagnie.*

# Homecoming—or not?

A happy homecoming to follow a successful cruise was the ambition of every auxiliary cruiser commander and crew. As the months passed, thoughts would dwell more and more on what life was going to be like: people, things, wishes and hopes; but first the British blockade had to be penetrated. The pros and cons of different routes had to be carefully considered. A commander's choice at this stage could decide the fate of the ship and crew with which he had been entrusted, as the case might be, by the First World War *Admiralstab* or the Second World War *Seekriegsleitung*.

Determination to see a joyful ending brought out the best in everyone. A fresh disguise would have to be adopted. As one neared home there would be neutral shipping around to offer a pattern, such as Spanish government vessels making for the French Atlantic coast. Tension and vigilance would increase from day to day. During the First World War auxiliary cruisers would normally arrive unheralded in home waters. If, however, one of them had been able to signal her impending landfall, she would be greeted enthusiastically as was the *Möwe* by the High Seas Fleet at the end of her first cruise. *Wolf* (II), however, was forced to maintain silence for fear of endangering the prize which was following her, the *Igotz Mendi*, but a few days later her crew were marching through Berlin's Brandenburg Gate to a tremendous reception in the

*During the last leg of her voyage home the* Widder *was disguised to represent the Spanish government steamer* Neptuno *of Bilbao. She trailed a steel hawser to which was attached a floating line.*

fourth springtime of the First World War.

Matters were different during the Second World War as ships could be reported when well away from land. Radio was the main link between the seafarer and those who waited for him at home, while ships' newspapers and bulletins had for some years taken the edge off his sense of isolation. An auxiliary cruiser's homecoming had to be kept secret for security reasons unless the 'powers that be' considered that broadcasting the story of her successes would be a boost to civilian morale. When a ship arrived in port her crew would have to leave what had become a second home to many. The *Möwe, Thor, Komet* and *Michel,* however, were each to set off on a second cruise, albeit with fresh commanders and part of their crews.

After both world wars, years were to elapse before all the auxiliary cruiser men returned home from internment or prisoner-of-war camps. Experiences aboard their interned or, more often, seized ships varied. Some are buried in foreign soil, the victims of tropical disease. Many had adventurous journeys home. Such was their lot before

they were able to tread German soil again.

How the *Stier*'s crew reached home has already been related, but the experiences of the *Atlantis'* men were very different. *U-126,* which they had been refuelling, took 55 men aboard. 52 camped on deck, their lifejackets permanently fastened against the possibility of being washed off or of the U-boat having to do a crash-dive. 201 men were accommodated in two launches and four whalers towed by the U-boat, which stated her intention of taking them to the coast of South America. The trip, it was estimated, would last 14 days. Two days later news arrived that three more submarines and the supply ship *Python* were being despatched to the scene.

*At the termination of her first cruise on March 4 1916,* Möwe *was met by units of the High Seas Fleet and escorted into Wilhelmshaven. The battlecruiser* Moltke *can be seen to the left and the* Derfflinger *to the extreme right. Two torpedo boats are visible between the* Möwe *and the latter. The commander-in-chief radioed to the* Möwe: *'With pride and joy the Fleet extends its heartfelt welcome!'*

**Left** *Crewmen from the* Cormoran *interned on Guam in 1915. When the United States entered the war, all German servicemen interned in the country became prisoners of war and their ships seized unless, as in the* Cormoran*'s case, they had already been sunk by their own crews.*

**Below** *Following the sinking of their ship, the crew of the* Atlantis *gather together in their Carley floats and whalers preparatory to an attempt to reach the nearest land.*

*December 23 1941, and the crew of* Atlantis *parade on the deck of the Italian submarine* Luigi Torelli *at St Nazaire to be addressed by Admiral Lindau,* Marinebefehlshaber *of Western France.*

The next day the men were taken aboard the *Python* but, before the voyage could properly begin, she was ordered to refuel the U-boats *U-68* and *UA* which she started to do on December 1 but, while they were there, a British 'County' Class cruiser appeared on the horizon. The *Python* tried to entice the cruiser towards the positions of the now-submerged U-boats. Five torpedoes fired from the *UA* at a range of 3,000 metres missed because her commander had underestimated the cruiser's speed, and with them went the *Python*'s last chance of escape. She faced the inevitable. As the first shells came over, her master decided to scuttle his ship.

With the *Python*'s civilian crew, 414 men had now to be returned home. Each of the U-boats had about 100 stowed inside literally like sardines, and was towing five lifeboats with life-rafts on deck which would float off with the remaining men should she have to crash-dive. The next day the *Python*'s crew were transferred to yet another U-boat. More U-boats and four Italian submarines arrived, thus freeing the men from the ordeal of hunger and thirst which they would have otherwise had to face in open boats, or that of being swamped in bad weather. Around Christmas 1941 the submarines arrived in Western France with their strange but valuable cargoes. After nearly one and three quarter years the men of the *Atlantis* were home.

There was to be no homecoming such as befitted the end of a cruise for the *Coronel*. At the start of her westward passage she had come under aerial attack and suffered damage forward. When she was attacked again, this time receiving a bomb in her stern—which, fortunately, did not explode—the *Seekriegsleitung* ordered the abandonment of this, her only venture. She had narrowly missed sharing the fate of the *Komet* which, on reaching a point further west, had been intercepted by British naval forces, damaged by shell fire and then sunk by a motor torpedo boat.

Further details of individual ships' careers and

their eventual fates are given in the summary on page 136.

When writing of the ships, their commanders and their crews, one should not forget those hundreds of other human beings who were as deeply involved with the fates of the auxiliary cruisers as were the men at sea themselves: their relatives. The departure of a husband, son, father, brother, friend or fiancé, followed by only irregular news, must have been a constant burden to all of them. Who can even attempt to visualise their hopes and prayers, their unceasing anxiety, or their despair when tidings of death reached home?

That the authorities always did what they might have done to ease the strain is shown by the accompanying facsimile of the *Seekriegsleitung*'s official notice telling of the *Michel*'s sinking on October 17 1943. One can hardly credit that, after more than six months, the fact that part of the crew had been rescued by the Japanese was still unknown in Berlin. A mixed experience was shared by the relatives of the crew of the auxiliary cruiser *Wolf* (II) who each received a formal notice on these lines through the post as the ship herself was sailing into Kiel. The next day's newspapers carried an announcement, couched in terms of all seriousness, that the notices had been 'overtaken by events'!

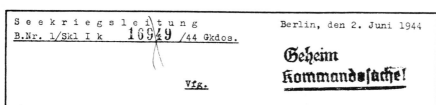

**Left** *The* Seekriegleitung*'s official notice telling of the* Michel*'s sinking on October 17 1943.*

**Below** *Pictured here as representative of all German auxiliary cruiser crewmen during the Second World War is a leading telegraphist, his identity unknown to the author. He proudly wears the auxiliary cruiser badge, a Viking ship sailing over the globe.*

**Above** *After over a year away from home, the* Wolf *returns to Kiel on February 24 1918. She flies a paying-off pennant while her aircraft* Wölfchen *circles overhead.*

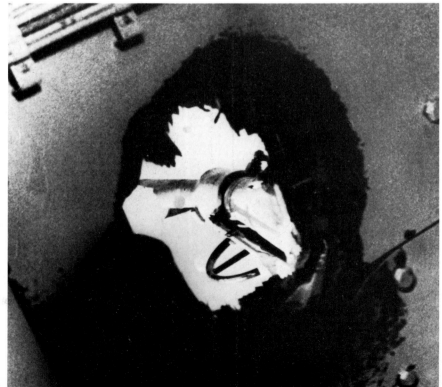

**Right** *A heavy bomb struck the auxiliary cruiser* Coronel *aft but did not explode. This photo was taken looking almost vertically through the hole to the damaged MG C/30 mounting.*

# Retrospect and prospect

For reasons already explained, no attempt has been made to compare the performances of auxiliary cruisers, either with each other or with their foreign equivalents; nor are the respective results achieved during each world war compared. The many imponderables of war at sea are not for this book, which has as its main aim the presentation of illustrations and tabulated data.

The table opposite shows a fixed relationship between the number of auxiliary cruisers in service and the number of ships sunk. The abscissa (horizontal) axis has two scales, the ordinate (vertical) axis only one!

One might follow a look back with a look ahead. To judge the possibilities for auxiliary cruiser usage in a future war one has to take into account the era of computers and satellites, and visualise the following:

A set of different kinds of sensors, electromagnetic, optical or acoustic, for instance, built into each ship and sensitive to the slightest perceptible impulse, which would operate on the IFF (Identification Friend or Foe) principle and, if necessary, not only trigger an alarm but also transmit within a fraction of a second the ship's position and the nature and bearing of the encountered impulse. Channelled into some sort of shipping control centre this data could be evaluated and a preliminary assessment of its importance flashed back. The anxious merchant ship master would then know within a few seconds the character of the vessel that had actuated his alarm signal.

A shore-based satellite system which would control all deep-sea shipping, consisting of sensors orbiting above the atmosphere and others beneath the surface of the sea. The coverage would be complete and no ship would be able to by-pass it.

Under these conditions, war on enemy commerce using ships relying solely on outward disguise would be impracticable. Only if a commerce raider could disguise her nature and intention from all the sensors at the same time would she stand any chance of success. The formalities required under the old system would go by the board: it would be pursuit to the point of sinking. Or will some power one day produce a navy with the technology to overcome these obstacles? What was it that used to be said about the German war-fleet? 'With God's help and the Navy, nothing is impossible!'

To-day's Federal German Navy *(Bundesmarine)* is concerned solely with the fulfilment of its role as an element in the North Atlantic Treaty Organisation, and this is restricted to the Baltic and North Sea. A commerce war in these waters is, in any case, unlikely. It can, and in fact must, therefore follow that no future German auxiliary cruisers are to be anticipated.

Let us then leave it at that, the German auxiliary cruisers taking their place in history as shining examples of gallantry, determination and inspiration for those navies which never possessed and will never possess them.

Diagram A
Number of auxiliary cruisers
in service and number of
sinkings during the Second
World War

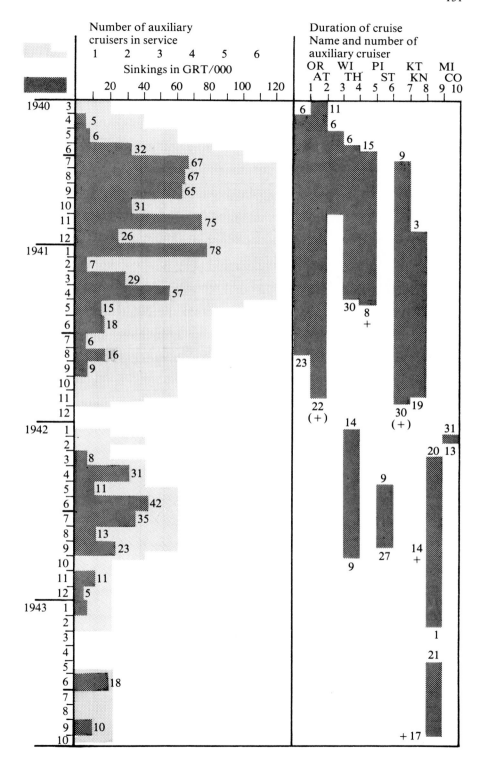

# Summary of commerce raiding by auxiliary cruisers, including related incidents

## The First World War

### 1914

Aug 2: *Kaiser Wilhelm der Große* commissioned as auxiliary cruiser. Sailed from Bremerhaven Aug 5.

Aug 3: *Victoria Luise* commissioned as auxiliary cruiser. Decommissioned Aug 8.

Aug 5: *Prinz Eitel Friedrich* commissioned as auxiliary cruiser in Tsingtao.

Aug 6: *Kronprinz Wilhelm* commissioned as auxiliary cruiser in mid-Atlantic by cruiser *Karlsruhe*.

Aug 7: *Cormoran* commissioned as auxiliary cruiser in Tsingtao.

Aug 26: *Kaiser Wilhelm der Große* sunk by own crew following engagement with British cruiser HMS *Highflyer*.

Aug 31: *Cap Trafalgar* commissioned as auxiliary cruiser off Trinidad Island by gunboat *Eber*.

Sep 14: *Cap Trafalgar* sunk in same area during engagement with armed merchant cruiser *Carmania*.

Sep 18: *Berlin* commissioned as auxiliary cruiser at Wilhelmshaven, principally for minelaying.

Oct 27: Battleship HMS *Audacious* sank after striking mine laid by *Berlin*.

Nov 18: *Berlin* interned at Trondheim.

Dec 13: *Cormoran* interned at Guam.

### 1915

Feb 8: Express steamer *Cap Polonio* commissioned as auxiliary cruiser *Vineta*. Decommissioned Feb 14.

Mar 10: *Prinz Eitel Friedrich* arrived at Newport News, USA, and interned.

Apr 11: *Kronprinz Wilhelm* arrived at Newport News, USA, and interned.

May 6: *Meteor* commissioned as auxiliary cruiser. First cargo vessel so converted. Laid mines off Archangel. War on enemy trade in Kattegat. Laid mines in Moray Firth.

Aug 9: *Meteor* sunk by own crew when about to be intercepted by British cruisers. Crew avoided being taken prisoner.

Aug 15: Oberleutnant zur See (reserve) Theodor Wolf (born Sep 24 1885, lost overboard from *U 73* Jan 16 1916) suggested a cargo vessel fitted out as

auxiliary cruiser. Recommended leading particulars: 4,600 GRT, crew 152, cruising range 38,000 nautical miles, cruising endurance 140 days.

Aug 30: Navy C in C advanced Wolf's proposal to *Admiralstab* who agreed that ship could be used also as minelayer in foreign waters. Choice of suitable vessel to combine both functions entrusted to Korvettenkapitän Graf zu Dohna-Schlodien who decided upon fruitship *Pungo*, destined to become auxiliary cruiser *Möwe*. Minelaying was in forefront of minds of Navy chiefs. On completion of orders to this effect commerce raiding was to be left to discretion of commander.

Nov 1: Orders issued for commissioning of auxiliary cruiser *Möwe*.

Dec 4: Steamer *Pungo* arrived at Wilhelmshaven for conversion.

Dec 29: Auxiliary cruiser *Möwe* sailed on first cruise, escorted from Elbe by *U 68*.

### 1916

Jan 1: *Möwe* laid 252 mines off Pentland Firth.

Jan 6: Pre-'Dreadnought' battleship HMS *King Edward VII* sunk after striking mine laid by *Möwe*.

Jan 14: Auxiliary cruiser *Wolf* (I) commissioned.

Jan 23: Auxiliary cruiser *Greif* commissioned.

Feb 26: *Wolf* (I) stranded in Lower Elbe. Taken out of service Feb 28.

Feb 29: *Greif* sank in northern North Sea after engagement with two armed merchant cruisers, a light cruiser and destroyers. Sank armed merchant cruiser *Alcantara*.

Mar 4: *Möwe* arrived at Wilhelmshaven.

May 16: Naval auxiliary *Jupiter* commissioned, later to become auxiliary cruiser *Wolf* (II).

Aug 24: *Möwe* sailed on second cruise.

Nov 29: *Jupiter* became auxiliary cruiser *Wolf* (II).

Nov 30: *Wolf* (II) sailed from Kiel.

Dec 2: Auxiliary cruiser *Seeadler* commissioned at Blexen. Sailed Dec 21.

### 1917

Jan 16: *Wolf* (II) laid mines off Cape Town, Jan 18 on Agulhas Bank, Feb 16 off Colombo.

Jan 19: Auxiliary cruiser *Leopard* commissioned.

Mar 10: Engaement between *Möwe* and British

steamer *Otaki*. Casualties on both sides. *Otaki* sunk.

Mar 16: *Leopard* sunk off Faroe Islands by British cruiser and armed boarding vessel. No survivors.

Mar 21: *Möwe* arrived at Kiel at end of second cruise.

Jun 25–28: *Wolf* (II) laid mines off Australia and New Zealand.

Aug 2: *Seeadler* stranded off island of Mopelia.

Sep 4–5: *Wolf* (II) laid mines in approaches to Singapore.

### 1918

Feb 21: *Wolf* (II) in German waters. Arrived at Kiel Feb 24.

## The auxiliary cruiser problem between the wars

### 1919

Jun 28: Treaty of Versailles. Every kind of preparation for war contrary to terms of treaty forbidden. In first instance no specific mention of commerce-raiding using auxiliary cruisers. On the other hand numerous private accounts appeared, notably *Seeteufel* by Felix Graf von Luckner, commander of *Seeadler;* and, undoubtedly the best informed, *Das schwarze Schiff* by Fritz Witschetzky, gunnery officer of the *Wolf* (II).

### 1935

Mar 16: German rearmament with introduction of universal compulsory military service. In upper echelons of Navy thinking began on use of commerce-destroying cruisers together with pocket battleships to prevent movement of reinforcements from North Africa in case of war with France. This primary aim during first days of hostilities. At same time there would be the task, using merchant vessels converted to commerce-protection cruisers, of relieving small number of German light cruisers with insufficient cruising range, possibly even replacing them in Atlantic. Accordingly two parallel concepts arose: commerce-protection and commerce-destroying cruisers, each abbreviated to HSK *(Handels-Schutz-Kreuzer* and *Handels-Stör-Kreuzer)*. They became one as war threatened with Great Britain.

### 1937

Publication of *Die deutschen Hilfskreuzer* as part of the official history of the war at sea *Der Krieg zur See 1914–1918*, compiled by Vizeadmiral (retired) von Manthey.

### 1938

Thoughts regarding preparation of ships to serve as auxiliary cruisers on lines of those of 1914–1918 war. With memories of unfortunate experiences during those years, instead of regarding every ship as potential auxiliary cruiser, list of particular ships drawn up to give reserve of suitable craft sufficient for forseeable requirements. Personnel of all ranks to be trained. Crews to be drawn principally from men who had served aboard German Navy's three sail training ships.

Reason for later classification of 'heavy' and 'light' auxiliary cruisers presumed up to this time only retrospective: all heavy auxiliary cruisers larger than 7,021 GRT, all light auxiliary cruisers smaller than 5,042 GRT. Armament as basis of comparison applicable only in case of regular and not auxiliary cruisers.

On outbreak of war both human and material forces mobilised: selection of suitable vessels, instructions to shipyards for their conversion, mustering of crews, supervision, instructions, commissioning, training and exercises, all directed to departure for operational areas.

## The Second World War
**Outstanding incidents during the campaign against enemy commerce waged by auxiliary cruisers during the Second World War**

### 1939

Sep 3: Outbreak of Second World War. Declaration of German blockade area off large sections of British and French coasts.

Oct 10: Pan-American conference declared neutrality zone about 300 sea miles wide off coasts of American countries not in war.

Nov 21: Great Britain extended blockade of German ports.

### 1940

Mar 9: Contrary to the laws and usages of war at sea, Great Britain decreed that exports of German coal to Italy should no longer be regarded as neutral cargo in neutral ships.

The 'first wave' of auxiliary cruisers was to be despatched, at as nearly the same time as possible, to operational areas. Staggering of departures to some extent, however, necessary to minimise risk of observation.

Mar 11: *Atlantis* sailed for Indian Ocean, *Orion* on Apr 6 sailed from Süder Piep (west coast of Schleswig-Holstein) for Pacific, *Widder* on May 6 from Bergen for the Atlantic, *Thor* on Jun 6 from Kiel for South Atlantic, *Pinguin* on June 15 from Gotenhafen (Gdynia) to Indian Ocean and *Komet* on Jul 9 from Bergen through European and Asiatic northern waters to Pacific.

Apr 7–9: *Orion* amid German and Allied operations during occupation of Norway.

Apr 24: To ease pressure on German forces in Norway, *Orion* received orders to cause diversion by holding up ships in North Atlantic. British ship *Haxby* so attacked sent in error signal RRRR ('I am being attacked by warship') instead of QQQQ ('I am being attacked by raider') thereby achieving better result for German side.

May 3: *Atlantis* sank British *Scientist* whose QQQQ let world know for first time that raider was at sea.

May 18: *Tropic Sea*, prize of *Orion,* scuttled on approach of enemy forces whereby Allies learned of existence of second auxiliary cruiser in Pacific.

Jun 6: *Thor* sailed.

Jun 13–14: *Orion* laid 238 mines off Auckland, New Zealand (first victim Jun 19).

Jun 15: *Pinguin* sailed.

Jun 22: French capitulation. French Channel and Atlantic coasts now at disposal of auxiliary cruisers.

Jul 3: *Komet* sailed.

Jul 18: Allies learned appearance details of raider for first time from released prisoners.

Aug 17: Germany declared complete blockade of British Isles.

Sep: Greenland taken under trusteeship of USA making outward passage by auxiliary cruisers more difficult.

Oct 7: *Pinguin* fitted out captured tanker *Storstad* as minelayer *Passat,* transferring 110 mines to her. As ship bound for Australia when intercepted, would arouse little or no suspicion in those waters.

Oct 20: German 'Far East combined fleet' (*Orion, Komet* and supply ship *Kulmerland*) announced intention of widening radius of action.

Oct 28–Nov 7: *Pinguin* laid mines off south and west coasts of Australia, likewise *Passat* between Oct 29 and Nov 1.

Oct 31: *Widder* arrived at Brest.

Dec 3: *Kormoran* sailed from Gotenhafen (Gdynia) as first ship of second wave of auxiliary cruisers. Followed by *Thor, Michel* and *Stier.*

Dec 5: *Thor* in sharp engagement with British armed merchant cruiser *Carnarvon Castle* which put into Montevideo with 32 dead and 82 wounded. *Thor* undamaged.

Dec 6: *Komet* came up with *Triona.* Following examination sank her, notwithstanding protest from accompanying *Orion. Komet*'s commander released part of *Triona* crew whereby British learned further details of German auxiliary cruiser operations.

Dec 23: Through intercepted radio traffic *Komet* learned of arrival of three phosphate ships in Nauru. Decision to attack and destroy discharging quays implemented on Dec 27. Damage estimated as equivalent of sinking of 40 phosphate-carrying ships.

## 1941

Jan 14: *Pinguin* achieved best day's work of all auxiliary cruisers. Captured two whale factory ships, one depot ship and 11 catchers.

Apr 4: *Thor* sank British armed merchant cruiser *Voltaire.*

Apr 30: *Thor* arrived at Hamburg.

May 8: *Pinguin* sunk by 'County' Class cruiser HMS *Cornwall.*

Jun 22: Germany commenced hostilities against Soviet Union.

Jul 7: USA took over hitherto British-occupied Iceland.

Aug 23: *Orion* arrived at Royan.

Sep 11: US Navy ordered by government to shoot first in event of confrontation with Axis powers.

Nov 19: *Kormoran* sank light cruiser HMAS *Sydney* but had to be abandoned because of damage received. Many of crew reached Australian coast.

Nov 22: *Atlantis* destroyed by 'County' Class cruiser HMS *Devonshire.* Crew taken aboard supply ship *Python* which was herself sunk on Dec 1 by 'County' Class cruiser HMS *Dorsetshire.* Crew reached France travelling on German and Italian U-boats.

Nov 30: *Komet* arrived at Hamburg.

Dec 8: Germany and Italy declared war on USA. Japanese bases now open to German auxiliary cruisers.

## 1942

Jan 14: *Thor* left Gironde on second cruise.

Jan 18: German-Italian-Japanese military co-operation. Active support agreed for German auxiliary cruisers.

Mar 9: *Michel* left Kiel. Mar 20 sailed from La Pallice.

Mar 23: *Thor* captured valuable British documents

from *Pagasitikos* which helped her sink ships on Mar 30, Apr 1 and 10.

May 22: *Stier* sailed from Royan. First sinking Jun 4.

Jun 4/6: Battle of Midway. Turning point in Pacific war.

Aug 1: *Michel* and *Stier* operated together until Aug 9.

Sep 27: *Stier* sank American cargo vessel *Stephen Hopkins* in fierce engagement but was herself abandoned and sunk. Crew picked up by supply ship *Tannenfels* and taken to France.

Oct 8: *Komet* sailed from Hamburg on seond cruise.

Oct 9: *Thor* on second cruise arrived at Yokohama.

Oct 14: *Komet* sunk off Cap de la Hague by British motor torpedo boat *236*. No survivors.

Nov 7/8: Allied landings in North Africa. War on enemy commerce in North Atlantic made increasingly difficult.

Nov 30: Devastating explosion aboard supply ship *Uckermark* at Yokohama. Auxiliary cruiser *Thor* and supply ship *Leuthen* burnt out.

**1943**

Jan 31: Auxiliary cruiser *Coronel* left Baltic for Norway, Feb 2 from Sylt, Feb 10 from Dunkirk, Feb 13 damaged by air attack off Boulogne, Feb 26 bombed again at Boulogne. Ordered back. Mar 2 arrived at Kiel.

Mar 1: *Michel* arrived at Yokohama.

May 21: *Michel* sailed from Yokohama on second cruise.

Sep 11: Last sinking of merchant ship by auxiliary cruiser. Helped by motorlaunch *LS 4*, *Michel* sank Norwegian tanker *India*.

Oct 12: Portugal allowed Allies use of Azores as air base.

Oct 17: *Michel* sunk by US submarine USS *Tarpon*. 116 survivors reached Japan. End of war on enemy commerce by German auxiliary cruisers.

# The fate of the auxiliary cruisers

**1** *Normannia:* 1898 Spanish auxiliary cruiser *Patriota,* 1899 French *L'Aquitaine,* 1906 broken up.

**2** *Kaiser Wilhelm der Große:* Aug 26 1914 badly damaged when attacked by British light cruiser HMS *Highflyer* after discovery refuelling at Spanish Rio de Oro. Sunk by own crew.

**3** *Cormoran:* Dec 13 1914 interned at Guam, Apr 7 1917 sunk by own crew to avoid seizure. Seven dead.

**4** *Prinz Eitel Friedrich:* Apr 9 1915 interned at Newport News USA, Apr 7 1917 seized and entered service as troopship *De Kalb.* 1921 *Mount Clay,* 1927 broken up.

**5** *Kronprinz Wilhelm:* Apr 26 interned at Newport News USA, Apr 17 1917 seized and entered service as troopship *von Steuben,* 1923 broken up.

**6** *Cap Trafalgar:* Sep 14 1914 sunk by armed merchant cruiser *Carmania* near Trinidad off coast of Brazil, 16 dead. Survivors interned in Argentina.

**7** *Berlin:* Nov 18 1914 interned at Trondheim, Norway, 1921 to Great Britain, *Arabic,* 1931 broken up.

**8** *Vineta:* Withdrawn from service following Feb 14 1915 trials as consequence of poor speed, *Cap Polonio.* 1919 to Great Britain, 1921 bought back by Hamburg South America Line, 1936 broken up.

**9** *Meteor:* Aug 9 1915 scuttled in North Sea on approach of five British cruisers.

**10** *Möwe:* Jun 12–Aug 24 1916 auxiliary cruiser *Vineta,* 1918 auxiliary minelayer *Ostsee,* 1919 to Great Britain, *Greenbrier.* 1933 to Germany, *Oldenburg.* Apr 7 1945 sunk off Norway by British submarine, 1953 wreck broken up.

**11** *Wolf* (I): Feb 26 1916 broke her back at mouth of Elbe while outward bound, withdrawn from service. 1919 to France.

**12** *Greif:* Feb 29 1916 sunk in northern North Sea following engagement with two armed merchant cruisers, light cruiser and destroyers. Of these armed merchant cruiser *Alcantara* sunk. 97 dead.

**13** *Wolf* (II): 1918 auxiliary cruiser in Baltic, 1919 to France, *Antinous.* 1931 broken up.

**14** *Seeadler:* Aug 2 1917 stranded on island of Mopelia (Society Islands), abandoned.

**15** *Geier:* Feb 14 1917 disarmed, sunk by *Möwe* as machinery worn out.

**16** *Leopard:* Mar 16 1917 sunk in action with armoured cruiser HMS *Achilles* and armed boarding vessel *Dundee* of Faroe Islands.

**17** *Iltis:* Mar 15 1917 scuttled on approach of British naval forces. Crew taken prisoner.

**18** *Orion:* 1942 repair ship, Jan 12 1944 gunnery training ship *Hektor,* from around turn of year 1944/45 again *Orion,* May 4 1945 sunk by British bombers north of Swinemünde, 1952 wreck broken up.

**19** *Atlantis:* Nov 23 1941 damaged by British 'County' Class cruiser HMS *Devonshire,* sunk by own crew who reached home.

**20** *Widder:* 1941 repair ship, 1945 British prize, 1946 *Ulysses,* 1950 German *Fechenheim,* Oct 3 1955 ashore in gale off coast of Norway, 1956 broken up.

**21** *Thor:* Nov 30 1942 badly damaged in Yokohama when supply ship *Uckermark* blew up. 12 dead. Withdrawn from service. Broken up.

**22** *Pinguin:* May 8 1941 sunk north of Seychelles by British 'County' Class cruiser HMS *Cornwall.* 341 dead. Survivors taken prisoner.

**23** *Stier:* Sep 27 1942 disabled in action with American cargo vessel *Stephen Hopkins.* Sunk by own crew. Four dead.

**24** *Komet:* Oct 14 1942 outward bound off Cap de la Hague (English Channel) when sunk by two torpedoes from British motor torpedo boat *236.*

**25** *Kormoran:* Nov 19 1941 disabled off west coast of Australia in action with Australian light cruiser HMAS *Sydney* which sank. Sunk by own crew, 76 dead.

**26** *Michel:* Oct 17 1943 sunk south of Yokohama by three torpedoes from submarine USS *Tarpon.* 290 dead. Survivors reached Japan.

**27** *Coronel:* Summer 1943 blockade runner, Oct 16 1943 night fighter direction ship *Togo,* Aug 13 1945 British prize, 1946 to USA, later Norwegian *Svalbard,* 1954 *Tilthorn,* 1955 *Stella Marina,* 1956 German *Togo,* 1968 *Lacasielle* Panama, 1976 renamed *Topeka,* 1979 still in service.

**28** *Hansa:* Target ship for U-boat training in Baltic, 1944 school and target ship, May 4 1945 mined in western Baltic, raised, British prize *Empire Humber,* 1946 *Glengarry,* 1970 *Dardanus,* 1971 *Glengarry,* broken up same year.

# Successes in the German auxiliary cruisers' commerce war

## Captured and/or sunk by German auxiliary cruisers in both world wars

| Nat. | Type | Name | GRT | Date | Remarks |
|---|---|---|---|---|---|

### Kaiser Wilhelm der Große
### 4.8.–26.8.1914

| Nat. | Type | Name | GRT | Date | Remarks |
|---|---|---|---|---|---|
| GB | F | Tubal Cain | 225 | 7.8.1914 | + |
| GB | F | Kaipara | 7,392 | 16.8.1914 | + |
| GB | F | Nyanga | 3,066 | 16.8.1914 | + |
| | | 3 ships | 10,683 | | |

### Prinz Eitel Friedrich
### 5.8.1914–10.3.1915

| Nat. | Type | Name | GRT | Date | Remarks |
|---|---|---|---|---|---|
| GB | F | Charcas | 5,067 | 5.12.1914 | + |
| F | S | Jean | 2,207 | 11.12.1914 | K,31.12. + |
| GB | S | Kildalton | 1,784 | 12.12.1914 | + |
| R | S | Isabel Browne | 1,315 | 26.1.1915 | + |
| F | S | Pierre Loti | 2,196 | 27.1.1915 | + |
| US | S | William P. Frye | 3,374 | 27.1.1915 | + |
| F | S | Jacobsen | 2,195 | 28.1.1915 | + |
| GB | S | Invercoe | 1,421 | 12.2.1915 | + |
| GB | F | Mary Ada Short | 3,605 | 18.2.1915 | + |
| F | F | Floride | 6,629 | 19.2.1915 | + |
| GB | F | Willerby | 3,630 | 20.2.1915 | + |
| | | 11 ships | 33,423 | | |

### Kronprinz Wilhelm
### 8.8.1914–11.4.1915

| Nat. | Type | Name | GRT | Date | Remarks |
|---|---|---|---|---|---|
| GB | F | Indian Prince | 2,846 | 4.9.1914 | K,9.9. + |
| GB | F | La Correntina | 8,528 | 7.10.1914 | 14.10 + |
| F | S | Union | 2,183 | 28.10.1914 | K,22.11. + |
| F | S | Anne de Brétagne | 2,063 | 21.11.1914 | 24.11. + |
| GB | F | Bellevue | 3,814 | 4.12.1914 | K,20.12. + |
| F | F | Mont Agel | 4,803 | 4.12.1914 | + |
| GB | F | Hemisphere | 3,486 | 28.12.1914 | K,8.1.1915 + |
| GB | F | Potaro | 4,419 | 28.12.1914 | K,8.1.1915 + |
| GB | F | Highland Brae | 7,634 | 14.1.1915 | K,30.1. + |
| GB | S | Wilfried M | 251 | 14.1.1915 | + |
| N | S | Semantha | 2,280 | 3.2.1915 | + |
| GB | F | Chasehill | 4,583 | 22.2.1915 | K, det. 9.3. |
| F | F | Guadeloupe | 6,600 | 23.2.1915 | 24.2. + |
| GB | F | Tamar | 3,207 | 24.3.1915 | + |
| GB | F | Coleby | 3,824 | 28.3.1915 | + |
| | | 15 ships | 60,522 | | |

### Meteor
### First cruise 29.5.– .6.1915

| Nat. | Type | Name | GRT | Date | Remarks |
|---|---|---|---|---|---|
| S | F | Verdandi | 950 | 15.6.1915 | + |
| N | F | Granit | 662 | 16.6.1915 | + |
| S | F | Thorsten | 1,634 | 16.6.1915 | P |
| | | 3 ships | 3,246 | | |

### Second cruise 6.8.–9.8.1915

| Nat. | Type | Name | GRT | Date | Remarks |
|---|---|---|---|---|---|
| GB | F | The Ramsey, ABV | 1,621 | 8.8.1915 | + × |
| DK | S | Jason | ? | 8.8.1915 | + |
| | | 2 ships | 1,621 | | |

### Möwe
### First cruise 29.12.1915–4.3.1916

| Nat. | Type | Name | GRT | Date | Remarks |
|---|---|---|---|---|---|
| GB | F | Corbridge | 3,687 | 11.1.1916 | K, 30.1. + |
| GB | F | Farringford | 3,146 | 11.1.1916 | + |
| GB | F | Dromonby | 3,627 | 13.1.1916 | + |
| GB | F | Author | 3,496 | 13.1.1916 | + |
| GB | F | Trader | 3,608 | 13.1.1916 | + |
| GB | F | Ariadne | 3,035 | 15.1.1916 | + |
| GB | F | Appam | 7,781 | 15.1.1916 | P, 17.1. det. |
| GB | E | Clan Mactavish | 5,816 | 16.1.1916 | + |
| GB | S | Edinburgh | 1,473 | 22.1.1916 | + |
| GB | F | Luxembourg | 4,322 | 4.2.1916 | + |
| GB | F | Flamenco | 4,540 | 6.2.1916 | + |
| GB | F | Westburn [1] | 3,300 | 8.2.1916 | P, 9.2. det. |
| GB | F | Horace | 3,109 | 9.2.1916 | + |
| F | F | Maroni | 3,109 | 24.2.1916 | + |
| GB | F | Saxon Prince | 3,471 | 25.2.1916 | + |
| | | 15 ships | 57,520 | | |

[1] 22.2 to Santa Cruz, Teneriffe; later sunk.

### As auxiliary cruiser Vineta in the Baltic

| Nat. | Type | Name | GRT | Date | Remarks |
|---|---|---|---|---|---|
| GB | F | Eskimo | 3,326 | 27.7.1916 | P |
| | | 1 ship | 3,326 | | |

### Möwe
### Second cruise 23.11.1916–22.3.1917

| Nat. | Type | Name | GRT | Date | Remarks |
|---|---|---|---|---|---|
| GB | F | Voltaire | 8,618 | 2.12.1916 | + |
| N | F | Hallbjörg | 2,586 | 4.12.1916 | + |
| GB | F | Mount Temple | 9,792 | 6.12.1916 | + |
| GB | S | Duchess of Cornwall | 152 | 8.12.1916 | + |
| GB | F | King George | 3,852 | 8.12.1916 | + |
| GB | F | Cambrian Range | 4,235 | 9.12.1916 | + |
| GB | F | Georgic | 10,077 | 10.12.1916 | + |
| GB | F | Yarrowdale | 4,652 | 11.12.1916 | [1]) |
| GB | F | Saint Theodore | 4,992 | 12.12.1916 | [2]) |
| GB | F | Drámatist | 5,415 | 18.12.1916 | + |
| F | S | Nantes | 2,679 | 26.12.1916 | + |
| F | S | Asnières | 3,103 | 2.1.1917 | + |
| JA | F | Hudson Maru | 3,798 | 5.1.1917 | det. |
| GB | F | Radnorshire | 4,310 | 8.1.1917 | + |
| GB | F | Minieh | 2,890 | 9.1.1917 | + |
| GB | F | Netherby Hall | 4,461 | 10.1.1917 | + |
| GB | F | Brecknockshire | 8,423 | 15.2.1917 | + |
| GB | F | French Prince | 4,766 | 16.2.1917 | + |

| GB | F | Eddie | 2,652 | 16.2.1917 | + |
| GB | F | Katherine | 2,926 | 24.2.1917 | + |
| GB | F | Rhodanthe | 3,061 | 4.3.1917 | + |
| GB | F | Esmeraldas | 4,678 | 10.3.1917 | + |
| GB | F | Otaki | 9,575 | 10.3.1917 | + × |
| GB | F | Demeterton | 6,048 | 13.3.1917 | + |
| GB | F | Governor | 5,524 | 14.3.1917 | + |
| | | 25 ships | 123,265 | | |

[1]) P, 31.12. Swinemünde, later auxiliary cruiser *Leopard*.
[2]) Later auxiliary *Geier*, 14.2.1917 ( + ).

## Greif
### 27.2.–29.2.1916

| GB | P | Alcantara, AMC | 15,620 | 29.2.1916 | + × |
| | | 1 ship | 15,620 | | |

## Wolf
### 30.11.1916–24.2.1918

| GB | F | Turritella | 5,528 | 27.1.1917 | [1]) |
| GB | F | Jumna | 4,152 | 1.3.1917 | K,3.3. + |
| GB | F | Wordsworth | 3,509 | 11.3.1917 | 18.3. + |
| GB | S | Dee | 1,169 | 30.3.1917 | + |
| GB | F | Wairuna | 3,947 | 2.6.1917 | K,17.6. + |
| US | S | Winslow | 567 | 16.6.1917 | K,22.6. + |
| US | S | Beluga | 507 | 9.7.1917 | 11.7. + |
| US | S | Encore | 651 | 14.7.1917 | + |
| GB | F | Matunga | 1,618 | 6.8.1917 | 26.8. + |
| JA | F | Hitachi Maru | 6,557 | 26.9.1917 | 7.11. + |
| SP | F | Igotz Mendi | 4,648 | 10.11.1917 | K [2]) |
| US | S | John H. Kirby | 1,296 | 30.11.1917 | 1.12. + |
| F | S | Maréchal Davout | 2,192 | 15.12.1917 | + |
| N | S | Storebror | 2,050 | 4.1.1918 | + |
| | | 14 ships | 38,391 | | |

[1]) Entered service 27.2.1917 as auxiliary cruiser *Iltis*, ( + ) on approach of British naval forces 15.3.1917.
[2]) Stranded off Skagen 24.2.1918.

## Seeadler
### 21.12.1916–2.8.1917

| GB | F | Gladis Royle | 3,268 | 9.1.1917 | + |
| GB | F | Lundy Island | 3,095 | 10.1.1917 | + |
| F | S | Charles Gounod | 2,199 | 21.1.1917 | + |
| GB | S | Percé | 364 | 24.1.1917 | + |
| F | S | Antonin | 3,071 | 3.2.1917 | + |
| I | S | Buenos Ayres | 1,811 | 9.2.1917 | + |
| GB | S | Pinmore | 2,431 | 19.2.1917 | + |
| GB | S | British Yeoman | 1,953 | 26.2.1917 | + |
| F | S | La Rochefoucauld | 2,200 | 27.2.1917 | + |
| F | S | Dupleix | 2,206 | 5.3.1917 | + |
| GB | F | Horngarth | 3,609 | 11.3.1917 | + |
| F | S | Cambronne | 1,833 | 21.3.1917 | [1]) |
| US | S | A.B. Johnson | 529 | 14.6.1917 | + |
| US | S | R.C. Slade | 673 | 18.6.1917 | + |
| US | S | Manila | 731 | 8.7.1917 | + |
| F | S | Lutèce | 126 | 5.9.1917 | [2]) |
| | | 16 ships | 30,099 | | |

[1]) Detached with prisoners to Rio de Janeiro 21.3., arrived 30.3.
[2]) Sailed by *Seeadler*'s chief officer from Mopelia to Easter Island as SMH (His Majesty's auxiliary cruiser) *Fortuna* with balance of *Seeadler*'s crew. Arrived 4.10 but sank there as result of leaky condition. Crew taken to Chile where interned.

## Geier
### 28.12.1916–14.2.1917

| GB | S | Jean | 215 | 31.12.1916 | + |
| N | S | Staut | 1,227 | 3.1.1917 | + |
| | | 2 ships | 1,442 | | |

## Orion
### 30.3.1940–23.8.1941

| GB | F | Haxby | 5,207 | 24.4.1940 | + |
| N | F | Tropic Sea | 8,750 | 19.6.1940 | P [1]) |
| F | F | Notou | 2,489 | 16.8.1940 | + |
| GB | F | Turakina | 9,691 | 20.8.1940 | + |
| N | F | Ringwood | 7,203 | 14.10.1940 | + |
| GB | F | Chaucer | 5,792 | 29.7.1941 | + |
| | | 6 ships | 39,132 | | |

[1]) Sunk by a British submarine shortly before reaching port.

## Orion and Komet together
### 25.11.–8.12.1940

| GB | F | Holmwood | 546 | 25.11.1940 | + |
| GB | P | Rangitane | 16,712 | 27.11.1940 | + |
| GB | F | Triona | 4,413 | 6.12.1940 | + |
| N | F | Vinni (KT) | 5,181 | 7.12.1940 | + |
| GB | F | Komata (KT) | 3,900 | 7.12.1940 | + |
| GB | F | Triadic (OR) | 6,378 | 8.12.1940 | + |
| GB | F | Triaster (OR) | 6,032 | 8.12.1940 | + |
| | | 7 ships | 43,162 | | |

## Komet
### Second cruise 9.7.1940–30.11.1941

| GB | F | Australind | 5,020 | 14.8.1941 | + |
| NL | F | Kota-Nopan | 7,322 | 17.8.1941 | P |
| GB | F | Devon | 9,036 | 19.8.1941 | + |
| | | 3 ships | 21,378 | | |

## Atlantis
### 11.3.1940–22.11.1941

| GB | F | Scientist | 6,199 | 3.5.1940 | + |
| N | F | Tirranna | 7,230 | 10.6.1940 | P [1]) |
| GB | F | City of Bagdad | 7,506 | 11.7.1940 | + |
| GB | F | Kemmendine | 7,770 | 13.7.1940 | + |
| N | F | Talleyrand | 6,732 | 2.8.1940 | + |
| GB | F | King City | 4,744 | 24.8.1940 | + |
| GB | T | Athelking | 9,557 | 9.9.1940 | + |
| GB | F | Benarty | 5,800 | 10.9.1940 | + |
| F | P | Commissaire Ramel | 10,061 | 20.9.1940 | + |
| YU | F | Durmitor | 5,623 | 22.10.1940 | P [2]) |

| | | | | | |
|---|---|---|---|---|---|
| N | T | Teddy | 6,748 | 9.11.1940 | + |
| N | T | Ole Jakob | 8,306 | 10.11.1940 | P ³) |
| GB | F | Automedon | 7,528 | 11.11.1940 | + |
| GB | F | Mandasor | 5,144 | 24'1'1941 | + |
| GB | F | Speybank | 5,154 | 31.1.1941 | P ⁴) |
| N | F | Ketty Brövig | 7,301 | 2.2.1941 | P ⁵) |
| AE | P | Zam Zam | 8,299 | 17.4.1941 | + |
| GB | F | Rabaul | 6,809 | 14.5.1941 | + |
| GB | F | Trafalgar | 4,530 | 24.5.1941 | + |
| GB | F | Tottenham | 4,762 | 17.6.1941 | + |
| GB | F | Balzac | 5,372 | 22.6.1941 | + |
| N | F | Silvaplana | 4,793 | 10.9.1941 | P ⁶) |
| | | 22 ships | 145,968 | | |

¹) Detached 5.8. Torpedoed off Gironde 22.9.
²) Detached 20.10.1940. Put into Mogadishu where taken by British when port occupied.
³) Detached 16.11.1940. Put into Yokohama. Arrived Bordeaux 19.7.1941.
⁴) Detached 21.3.1941. Reached Gironde 10.5. Later served as minelayer and blockade runner *Doggerbank*.
⁵) Captured by enemy forces 5.3.1941.
⁶) Detached 27.9.1941. Reached Boulogne 17.11.

## Widder
### 6.5.–31.10.1940

| | | | | | |
|---|---|---|---|---|---|
| GB | T | British Petrol | 6,891 | 13.6.1940 | + |
| N | T | Krosfonn | 9,323 | 26.6.1940 | P |
| GB | F | Davisian | 6,433 | 10.7.1940 | + |
| GB | F | King John | 5,228 | 13.7.1940 | + |
| N | T | Beaulieu | 6,114 | 4.8.1940 | + |
| NL | F | Oostplein | 5,059 | 8.8.1940 | + |
| SF | S | Killoran | 1,817 | 10.8.1940 | + |
| GB | F | Anglo Saxon | 5,596 | 21.8.1940 | + |
| GB | T | Cymbeline | 6,317 | 2.9.1940 | + |
| GR | F | Antonios Chandris | 5,866 | 8.9.1940 | + |
| | | 10 ships | 58,644 | | |

## Thor
### First cruise 6.6.1940–30.4.1941

| | | | | | |
|---|---|---|---|---|---|
| NL | F | Kertosono | 9,289 | 1.7.1940 | P¹) |
| GB | F | Delambre | 7,032 | 7.7.1940 | + |
| B | F | Bruges | 4,983 | 9.7.1940 | + |
| GB | F | Gracefield | 4,631 | 14.7.1940 | + |
| GB | F | Wendover | 5,489 | 16.7.1940 | + |
| NL | F | Tela | 3,777 | 17.9.1940 | + |
| N | WK | Kosmos | 17,801 | 26.9.1940 | + |
| GB | F | Natia | 8,715 | 8.10.1940 | + |
| S | F | Trolleholm | 5,047 | 25.3.1941 | + |
| GB | P | Britannia | 8,799 | 25.3.1941 | + |
| GB | P | Voltaire, AMC | 13,245 | 4.4.1941 | + |
| S | F | Sir Ernest Cassel | 7,739 | 16.4.1941 | + |
| | | 12 ships | 96,547 | | |

¹) 12.7.1940 Arrived Lorient.

### Second cruise 14.1.–9.10.1942

| | | | | | |
|---|---|---|---|---|---|
| GB | F | Pagasitikos | 3,492 | 23.3.1942 | + |
| GB | F | Wellpark | 4,649 | 30.3.1942 | + |
| GB | F | Willesden | 4,563 | 1.4.1942 | + |
| N | F | Aust | 5,630 | 3.4.1942 | + |
| GB | F | Kirkpool | 4,842 | 10.4.1942 | + |
| GB | F | Nankin | 7,131 | 10.5.1942 | P¹) |
| NL | T | Olivia | 6,307 | 14.6.1942 | + |
| N | T | Herborg | 7,892 | 19.6.1942 | P²) |
| N | T | Madrono | 5,894 | 4.7.1942 | P³) |
| GB | F | Indus | 5,187 | 20.7.1942 | + |
| | | 10 ships | 55,587 | | |

¹) 18.7 arrived Japan. Later storeship *Leuthen*.
²) To Japan, later blockade runner *Hohenfriedberg*.
³) To Japan, later supply ship *Rossbach*.

## Pinguin
### 15.6.1940–8.5.1941

| | | | | | |
|---|---|---|---|---|---|
| GB | F | Domingo de Larrinaga | 5,358 | 31.7.1940 | + |
| N | T | Filefjell | 6,901 | 27.8.1940 | + |
| GB | T | British Commander | 5,008 | 27.8.1940 | + |
| N | F | Morviken | 7,616 | 27.8.1940 | + |
| GB | F | Benavon | 5,872 | 12.9.1940 | + |
| N | F | Nordvard | 4,111 | 16.9.1940 | P¹) |
| N | T | Storstad | 8,998 | 7.10.1940 | P²) |
| GB | F | Nowshera | 7,920 | 19.11.1940 | + |
| GB | F | Maimoa | 10,123 | 20.11.1940 | + |
| GB | F | Port Brisbane | 8,739 | 21.11.1940 | + |
| GB | F | Port Wellington | 8,303 | 30.11.1940 | + |
| N | WK | Ole Wegger | 12,201 | 14.1.1941 | P³) |
| N | WD | Solglimt | 12,246 | 14.1.1941 | P³) |
| N | WF | Pol VII | 336 | 14.1.1941 | P³) |
| N | WF | Pol VIII | 298 | 14.1.1941 | P³) |
| N | WF | Pol IX | 354 | 14.1.1941 | P⁴) |
| N | WF | Pol X | 354 | 14.1.1941 | P³) |
| N | WK | Pelagos | 12,083 | 14.1.1941 | P³) |
| N | WF | Star XIV | 247 | 14.1.1941 | P⁵) |
| N | WF | Star XIX | 249 | 14.1.1941 | P³) |
| N | WF | Star XX | 249 | 14.1.1941 | P³) |
| N | WF | Star XXI | 298 | 14.1.1941 | P³) |
| N | WF | Star XXII | 303 | 14.1.1941 | P³) |
| N | WF | Star XXIII | 357 | 14.1.1941 | P³) |
| N | WF | Star XXIV | 361 | 14.1.1941 | P⁵) |
| GB | F | Empire Light | 6,828 | 25.4.1941 | + |
| GB | F | Clan Buchanan | 7,266 | 28.4.1941 | + |
| GB | T | British Emperor | 3,663 | 7.5.1941 | + |
| | | 28 ships | 136,642 | | |

¹) 3.12.1940 arrived Bordeaux.
²) Became auxiliary minelayer *Passat*. 4.2.1941 arrived Gironde.
³) To Bordeaux.
⁴) Commissioned by *Komet* as minelayer *Adjutant*, 1.7.1941 (+).
⁵) 13.3.1941 (+) on approach of enemy forces.

## Stier
### 9.5.–27.9.1942

| Nat. | Type | Name | GRT | Date | |
|---|---|---|---|---|---|
| GB | F | Gemstone | 4,986 | 4.6.1942 | + |
| PA | T | Stanvac Calcutta | 10,170 | 6.6.1942 | + |
| GB | F | Dalhousie | 7,072 | 9.8.1942 | + |
| US | F | Stephen Hopkins | 8,500 | 27.9.1942 | + |
| | | 4 ships | 30,728 | | |

## Kormoran
### 3.12.1940–19.11.1941

| Nat. | Type | Name | GRT | Date | |
|---|---|---|---|---|---|
| GR | F | Antonis | 3,729 | 6.1.1941 | + |
| GB | T | British Union | 6,987 | 18.1.1941 | + |
| GB | F | Africa Star | 11,900 | 29.1.1941 | + |
| GB | F | Eurylochus | 5,723 | 29.1.1941 | + |
| GB | T | Agnita | 3,552 | 22.3.1941 | + |
| GB | T | Canadolite | 11,309 | 25.3.1941 | P [1]) |
| GB | F | Craftsman | 8,022 | 9.4.1941 | + |
| GR | F | Nicolas D.L. | 5,486 | 12.4.1941 | + |
| YU | F | Velebit | 4,153 | 26.6.1941 | + |
| GB | F | Mareeba | 3,472 | 26.6.1941 | + |
| GR | F | Stamatios G. Embiricos | 3,941 | 26.9.1941 | + |
| | L Cru | Sydney | – | 19.11.1941 | + |
| | | 11 ships | 68,274 | | |

[1]) 13.4.1941 arrived Gironde.

## Michel
### First cruise 20.3.1942–1.3.1943

| Nat. | Type | Name | GRT | Date | |
|---|---|---|---|---|---|
| GB | T | Patella | 7,468 | 19.4.1942 | + |
| US | T | Connecticut | 8,684 | 22.4.1942 | + |
| N | F | Kattegat | 4,245 | 20.5.1942 | + |
| US | F | George Clymer | 7,176 | 7.6.1942 | + |
| GB | F | Lylepark | 5,186 | 11.6.1942 | + |
| GB | P | Gloucester Castle | 8,006 | 15.7.1942 | + |
| US | T | William F. Humphrey | 7,893 | 16.7.1942 | + |
| N | T | Aramis | 7,984 | 17.7.1942 | + |
| GB | F | Arabistan | 5,874 | 14.8.1942 | + |
| GB | F | Empire Dawn | 7,241 | 10.9.1942 | + |
| US | F | American Leader | 6,778 | 11.9.1942 | + |
| GB | F | Reynolds | 5,113 | 2.11.1942 | + |
| US | F | Sawokla | 5,882 | 29.11.1942 | + |
| GR | F | Eugenie Livanos | 4,816 | 8.12.1942 | + |
| GB | F | Empire March | 7,040 | 2.1.1943 | + |
| | | 15 ships | 99,386 | | |

### Second cruise 21.5.–17.10.1943

| Nat. | Type | Name | GRT | Date | |
|---|---|---|---|---|---|
| N | F | Hoegh Silverdawn | 7,715 | 15.6.1943 | + |
| N | T | Ferncastle | 9,940 | 17.6.1943 | + |
| N | T | India | 9,977 | 11.9.1943 | + |
| | | 3 ships | 27,632 | | |

# Successes achieved through mines laid by auxiliary cruisers (sinkings only)

## First World War

| Nat. | Type | Name | GRT | Date | Approximate location of sinking |
|---|---|---|---|---|---|

### Berlin

| Nat. | Type | Name | GRT | Date | Location |
|---|---|---|---|---|---|
| GB | F | Manchester Commerce | 5,363 | 26.10.1914 | Irish Sea |
| GB | Bat | Audacious | 27,000 | | Irish Sea |
| | | 2 ships | 32,363 | | |

### Meteor

| Nat. | Type | Name | GRT | Date | Location |
|---|---|---|---|---|---|
| RU | F | ? | ca. 800 | 7.6.1915 | Archangel |
| RU | F | ? | ca. 5,000 | 7.6.1915 | Archangel |
| RU | F | ? | ca. 5,000 | 7.6.1915 | Archangel |
| | | 3 ships | ca. 10,800 | | |

### Möwe
#### First cruise

| Nat. | Type | Name | GRT | Date | Location |
|---|---|---|---|---|---|
| GB | Bat | King Edward VII | 16,350 | 6.1.1916 | Scotland |
| SP | F | Bayo | 2,776 | 13.1.1916 | Gironde |
| SP | F | Belgica | 2,068 | 15.1.1916 | Gironde |
| | | 3 ships | 21,194 | | |

### Wolf

| Nat. | Type | Name | GRT | Date | Location |
|---|---|---|---|---|---|
| GB | F | Matheran | 7,654 | 26.1.1917 | Cape Town |
| GB | F | Cilicia | 3,750 | 12.2.1917 | Cape Town |
| SP | F | C. de Fizaguirre | 4,376 | 26.5.1917 | Cape Town |
| GB | F | City of Athens | 5,604 | 10.8.1917 | Cape Town |
| GB | F | Worcestershire | 7,175 | 17.2.1917 | Colombo |
| GB | F | Perseus | 6,728 | 21.2.1917 | Colombo |
| JA | F | Unkai Maru | 2,143 | 16.6.1917 | Bombay |
| GB | F | Mongolia | 9,505 | 24.6.1917 | Bombay |
| GB | F | Okhla | 5,288 | 29.7.1917 | Bombay |
| GB | F | Croxteth Hall | 5,872 | 17.11.1917 | Bombay |
| GB | F | Wimmera | 3,622 | 26.6.1918 | Australia |
| GB | F | Cumberland | 9,471 | 6.7.1917 | Australia |
| GB | F | Port Kembla | 4,700 | 18.9.1917 | New Zealand |
| | | 13 ships | 75,888 | | |

## Second World War

### Orion

| Nat. | Type | Name | GRT | Date | Location |
|---|---|---|---|---|---|
| GB | P | Niagara | 13,415 | 19.6.1940 | New Zealand |
| GB | F | Puriri (auxiliary minesweeper) | 927 | | New Zealand |
| GB | F | Port Bowen | 8,276 | | New Zealand |
| GB | F | Baltanic | ca. 1,500 | | New Zealand |
| | | 4 ships | 24,118 plus 2 trawlers | | |

### *Pinguin* and *Passat*

| GB | F | Nimbin | 1,052 | Australia |
|----|----|--------|-------|-----------|
| GB | Fi | Millimumul | 287 | Australia |
| GB | F | Cambridge | 10,846 | Australia |
| US | F | City of Rayville | 5,883 | Australia |
| | | 4 ships | 18,068 | |

# German auxiliary cruisers which did not achieve any direct successes in the commerce war

| *Cap Trafalgar* | 4.8.–26.8.1914 |
|-----------------|----------------|
| *Cormoran* | 7.8.–13.12.1914 |
| *Berlin* | 16.10.–17.11.1914 |
| *Leopard* | 10.3.–16.3.1917 |
| *Coronel* | 13.2.1943 operation broken off |

# Tonnage comparisons of ships attacked by German raiders

## 1 Examples showing the average size of ships sunk by individual auxiliary cruisers in both world wars

| First World War | Number | GRT | Second World War | Number | GRT |
|-----------------|--------|-----|------------------|--------|-----|
| *Möwe* (first cruise) | 14 | 3,553 | *Atlantis* | 16 | 6,722 |
| *Wolf* (II) | 12 | 2,351 | *Kormoran* | 10 | 5,696 |

## 2 Total successes achieved by auxiliary cruisers in both world wars

| | First World War | | Second World War | |
|---|---|---|---|---|
| | Number | GRT | Number | GRT |
| Sunk | 96 | 332,957 | 101 | 657,801 |
| Sent home as prizes | 7 | 24,906 | 30 | 158,362 |
| Released/detached with prisoners | 5 | 21,295 | — | — |
| Warships sunk | — | — | 1 | 6,830 |
| *Total* | *108* | *379,158* | *132* | *823,080* |
| | | | | |
| **Sunk by mines** | | | | |
| Merchant vessels | 19 | 99,283 | 10 | 42,786 |
| Warships | 2 | 43,350 | — | — |

## 3 Ships taken prize and later lost

| | | | | |
|---|---|---|---|---|
| Sunk by enemy | — | — | 2 | 15,980 |
| Scuttled to prevent capture | — | — | 2 | 608 |
| Lost by marine peril | 1 | 4,648 | — | — |
| Sunk in action | — | — | 2 | 12,924 |
| Captured by enemy | — | — | 6 | 29,514 |

## 4 Total number and tonnage of attacked ships and their average GRT

| First World War | | | Second World War | | |
|---|---|---|---|---|---|
| Number | Tonnage | Average GRT | Number | Tonnage | Average GRT |
| 108 | 379,158 | 3,511 | 132 | 823,080 | 6,235 |

# Summary of source material

## Developments up to 1914

Various volumes of "Nauticus".—yearbook of 'Deutschlands Seeinteressen'. E.S. Mittler & Sohn, Berlin, from 1898.

Weyher, Bruno: "Taschenbuch der Kriegsflotten", from volume I, 1900.

The Belgian Shiplover—Bimonthly Organ of the Belgian Nautical Research Association, Brussels (various issues).

Kludas, Arnold: "Deutschlands erste Zweischrauben-Schnelldampfer", in: "Stallings maritimes Jahrbuch 1975/1976".

Militärarchiv Freiburg, documents.

## The First World War

Der Krieg zur See 1914–1918. "Der Kreuzerkrieg in den ausländischen Gewässern", compiled by Eberhard von Mantey, Berlin 1937.

Der Krieg zur See 1914–1918. "Die Überwasserstreitkräfte und ihre Technik", Berlin 1930.

Dohna-Schlodiehn, Nikolaus Graf und Burggraf zu: "Der *Möwe* Fahrten und Taten", Stuttgart and Gotha 1927.

Busch, Fritz Otto, and Forstner, Georg Frhr. von: "Krieg auf 7 Ozeanen", Berlin 1935.

Langsdorff, Werner von "Kaperkrieg im Atlantik—Taten deutscher Hilfskreuzer und Hilfsschiffe", Gütersloh 1938.

Mielke, Otto: "Im Gefolge des Kreuzergeschwaders—S.M. Hilfskreuzer *Prinz Eitel Friedrich*" SOS-Schicksale deutscher Schiffe, 1958.

*Witschetzky, Fritz:* "Das Schwarze Schiff—Hilfskreuzer *Wolf*".

Luckner, Graf Felix von: "Seeteufel—Abenteuer aus meinem Leben", Berlin and Leipzig 1926.

Militärarchiv Freiburg, documents.

## The Second World War

Assmann, Kurt: "Deutsche Schicksalsjahre", Brockhaus Wiesbaden 1950.

Brennecke, Jochen: "Gespensterkreuzer HK 33 (Hilfskreuzer *Pinguin*)" Deutscher Seeverlag, Hamm 1953.

Brennecke, Jochen: "Das große Abenteuer—Deutsche Hilfskreuzer 1939/45", Koehler, Biberach 1959.

Detmers, Theodor: "*Kormoran*—Der Hilfskreuzer, der die *Sydney* versenkte", Koehler, Biberach 1959.

Gröner, Erich: "Die deutschen Kriegsschiffe 1815–1945", J.F. Lehmann, München 1966/68.

Lohmann, Walter und Hildebrand, Hans H.: "Die deutsche Kriegsmarine 1939–1945", Podzun, Bad Nauheim 1956–1964.

O.K.M./3.S.K.L.: "Die Handelsflotten der Welt 1942", M.Dv. Nr. 135 (compiled by Erich Gröner).

O.K.M.: "Minenbedienungsvorschrift (M.B.V.)", secret M.Dv. Nr. 175, 1944.

Militärarchiv Freiburg, documents.

# Index